The Science of Breaking Out of Your Comfort Zone:
How to Live Fearlessly, Seize Opportunity, and Make Each Day Memorable

By Peter Hollins, Author and Researcher at petehollins.com

Table of Contents

Introduction

My hair was flying everywhere and my eyes were starting to dry out behind the tight goggles strapped to my head.

I was standing on an airplane, about to jump off, with only a man and a parachute strapped to my back. I was terrified of heights; how did I end up here?

We have to rewind the tape a few years to when I first met a girl named Sandra. We had a brief flirtation, and we seemed to have terrible timing, because as soon as I'd be available and single, she wouldn't, and vice versa. This dance went on for a while until that fateful summer when we were both seemingly available and ready to mingle.

I was less introverted than I was as a teenager, but compared to Sandy, I was a downright bookworm. She was extremely adventurous and thrill-seeking, often appearing to do things just for the sake of doing them. To be honest, I probably said no more out of habit and fear than anything else, so I admired her spirit and how many interesting situations it got her into.

You can see where this is going. I saw a part of her I admired and I liked her a lot, so when she suggested that we go skydiving to kick off the summer, I readily agreed. I agreed quickly as if I had been contemplating a similar stunt for years, and we set a date. If nothing else, I figured this experience would bond us together for the rest of my short life as I plummeted to my death.

To say that skydiving was out of my comfort zone was a bit of an understatement.

But as you can sense, all the motivations were there for me. I knew what I wanted from this experience (potential relationship with Sandra, cool pictures), and those were strong positive motivators—*carrots*, in popular terms. I also knew what the costs would be if I didn't jump on this opportunity and how much I would regret not simply sucking it up for, in reality, just a few minutes—these were the *sticks*. I had a very clear sense of my *whys*, and so into the plane I went. I wasn't so focused on the fear itself as I was on what was waiting for if I did or did not act. Sandra was suitably impressed, and we dated for the summer until we realized we had idealized each other for years and weren't actually such a good match.

We all have comfort zones for a reason.

They are necessary to growing our sense of confidence and showing vulnerability. They make us feel secure and safe, like heaping on blankets to ward off the cold (or monsters under the bed). And yet, if we stayed in the safe cocoon of our bed for our lives, what would we experience? What would we achieve? What would be the epitaph written on our tombstones?

Those questions all have the same answer: nothing.

Everything we want in life is squarely outside of our comfort zones—some closer, and some further outside. Growth, learning, and progress are outside. So are accomplishment, fulfillment, and satisfaction. They lie over the obstacles of fear, anxiety, and the unknown. The comfort zone for most people isn't about comfort; it's about retreating from fear and the fear of failure.

Sometimes, all it takes is the proper motivation to exit the comfort zone and grab what you want. I clearly had some powerful motivation to jump off a plane for

Sandra, but that's not necessarily something we can harness in daily life.

The Science of Breaking Out of Your Comfort Zone isn't just a pithy title with anecdotes about my checkered dating history. I wrote this book to be a detailed look into why we tend to stay in our comfort zones, what keeps us there, and what it really takes to break out and live the exact life you want. Often, we have told ourselves a story so often that it practically becomes true and you can't see a different version of your life.

It's almost certainly free and available— there's nothing keeping you from it except yourself.

Chapter 1. What Zone Do You Live In?

We are creatures of comfort. Most of us covet familiarity in our lives. The more we settle into a certain mood or situation, the more we know about how to act and what to do. This is a good feeling. We condition ourselves against disruption or surprise and favor environments where we know what to expect.

The place we go to soothe and relieve ourselves is called the "comfort zone." Everyone has a different definition of what occupies that space. The comfort zone is a virtual place in our minds.

Your comfort zone might be populated by longtime friends who console and amuse you or family members you're close with. It could be a coffee shop or park you regularly visit. In terms of work, your comfort zone could be routine tasks that you execute easily or a state where operations are running normally with no issues.

Our psychological, emotional, and behavioral inclinations inform what the comfort zone looks and feels like, determined by any number of measures: our habitats, topics of expertise, skill sets, or overall frames of mind. The security we feel in these specific realms can't always be replicated in other areas of our lives, and thus we tend to stay inside our comfort zones.

But the entire concept of the comfort zone is illusory: it's all in our heads. It's an intangible product of our desires, a fantasy that's actually achievable. Familiarity reinforces safety, and the comfort zone thrives on regular, routine habits in which we always know what we're doing. We are always confident and empowered in a comfort zone—there's little risk, if any. Our stress and anxiety levels are low, and we're generally happy and self-assured.

The refuge of the comfort zone, where routine reigns and dangers are low, can be a soothing, serene, and occasionally necessary mindset for us.

But it's also necessary for us to break out of it. Absolutely everything you want in life lies outside of it.

The Yerkes–Dodson Curve

The concept of the comfort zone has roots in one of the most notable behavioral experiments of the 20th century. In 1908, psychologists Robert M. Yerkes and John D. Dodson tested how sudden increases in arousal affected a person's level of productivity. The rather coarse (and admittedly unkind) trial involved the scientists applying small electric shocks to laboratory mice in a maze to show how that stress affected their efforts to get out of the maze.

Their findings resulted in a law, popularly represented by the Yerkes–Dodson curve.

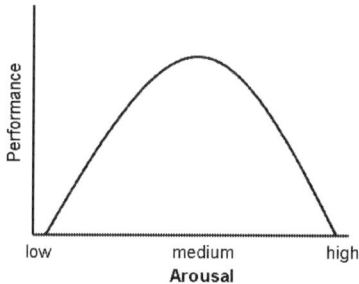

This graph shows the relationship between a subject's being "aroused" or stressed over a given task and their level of performance of the task. Perhaps unsurprisingly, low levels of arousal or pressure result in low performance levels. This makes some sense: if the tension of motivation is at a low point, one has no incentive to act.

As stimulation kicks in and arousal levels increase, then the level of performance does as well—to a point. When tension levels get too high, perhaps because of anxiety or over-distraction, performance starts to decrease.

The Yerkes–Dodson curve compares to a very simple illustration by Dan Blewett:

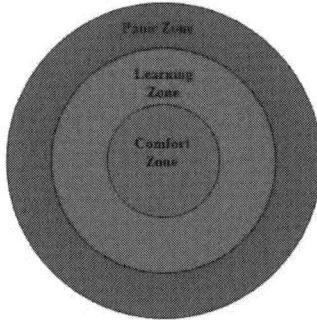

Here, the comfort zone is represented as a safe, centered spot. By moving outside the innermost circle to a spot with more stimulation, the subject is actively learning and applying mental energy to the task. Taking it too far too quickly, though, produces intense anxiety and panic, which for the vast majority of us are conditions that make work difficult.

The implications are fairly clear with both graphs. When we're cozy and contented, we're generally too relaxed to get much accomplished. While relaxation is always important, if we're too comfortable we stop growing and stop exerting effort, and this

17

opens the door to bad habits. Without stimulation, ambition and performance disappear.

On the other hand, pushing too much also lessens one's performance, as we move past mere arousal and into a frantic state. In this situation, we feel discouraged and distracted. Those feelings, in turn, open up the possibility of failure as a sort of relief—we just want to give up. Responding to our natural tendencies, we then seek refuge back in our neutral, safe comfort zone. Certainly, this shows how hard it is to get out of that tranquil place and take on new challenges.

The middle ground, where aroused tension exists but is still manageable, is a space called "optimal anxiety"—just a small step outside the comfort zone. This is where performance is maximized by being just stressed enough to increase execution, but not so distressed that we can't be productive. By pushing ourselves into that middle ground, we increase both the rate and quality of our accomplishments without overkill.

Take the extreme example of some of the most stressed-out workers in the world: air traffic controllers. They can't have a relaxed attitude about their work. They have to know the status of incoming and outgoing flights, weather conditions, and external factors in order to execute their responsibilities and ensure the safety of airline employees and passengers. A healthy amount of anxiety and concern gives them the ability to project those factors clearly and advise pilots of conditions. But letting their anxieties spin out unmanaged could cause confusion, lack of clarity, and a decrease in overall performance—and therefore a potentially tragic ending.

Inside and Outside the Comfort Zone

Lest we sound too hard on it, let's make sure we make one thing clear: there's nothing wrong with having a comfort zone. In fact, there's nothing inherently good *or* bad about the comfort zone. Gravitating toward it is part of our natural state, just as we're oriented to sleep at certain times.

Departing from it amplifies risk and anxiety, which likewise can be positive or negative. But for true growth and accomplishment, that's exactly what we have to do.

For some, the rewards of taking a chance aren't enough to get outside the comfort zone. They're satisfied with where they are and feel completely fulfilled in that state of contentment. But for someone who wants to advance and develop themselves, staying inside the comfort zone won't be satisfying at all.

For example, an Internet blogger might earn a respectable income churning out simple, easily digested captions, quotes, and quick articles for a website. They may, however, have a desire to write something longer and more substantial, like a novel. But taking the time and making the effort to devote energy toward that novel could be complicated by several factors: self-doubt, feelings of unworthiness, a cramped schedule, or concerns about how much research they'll need to do. To alleviate those fears, they simply stay in their workday rut where it's safe and quiet. But by choosing to remain static in their comfort zone, they become dissatisfied and miserable, asking themselves "what if?" over and over.

It's still necessary to *have* a comfort zone. There's nothing at all wrong with spending occasional time there, because we all need to relax and just "be" from time to time. That's all well and good. You can't jump into the deep end continually, day after day. Not only will you burn out quickly, but you'll become discouraged because your feelings of progress will transform into fatigue and displeasure and turn everything into a chore. Just as the elite athlete must rest during training periods, so must you rest. Retreating into the comfort zone from time to time isn't merely rest—it's necessary *recovery*.

The problem comes when we allow ourselves to get *too* settled in a comfort zone. After a certain time in that static mode, you stop trying to accomplish your aims, you stop challenging yourself, and you become too satisfied and docile. It's during that "waking sleep" that opportunities start to slip away.

The only sure way to increase growth, develop new talents and aptitude, and reach your true potential is by breaking out of that secure spot.

You shouldn't morph into an adrenaline junkie who can't get enough stimulus; you *should* become excited to learn what you're good at and develop new skills. That's another reason the comfort zone isn't a bad thing—you *will* need to come down and recharge at some point. And when you're headed back to the comfort zone, hopefully you'll have gained inspiration and creativity from your time *outside* it in that effective, productive, slightly stressful state of controlled disquiet.

Your Brain Likes Risks

Your brain responds positively to comfort, of course, by releasing the "happy" chemicals dopamine and serotonin. Those neurochemicals, combined with a lack of fear, is what keeps many of us from ever taking action. But scientists have also discovered that your brain also enjoys and rewards more stimulating and novel activities—the world that is outside your comfort zone.

New research from Vanderbilt psychology professor David Zald reveals that dopamine also kicks in during scary situations—and for some, the kick is bigger than comfortable situations. Zald says the brains of many people don't have what he calls "brakes" on the release and consumption of dopamine in the brain. This means that some really enjoy being in thrilling or risky situations. Part of that enjoyment could be related to self-esteem, a sense of accomplishment. While self-scaring isn't necessarily for all of us, those who enjoyed the rush of perilous encounters felt a profound effect.

Zald also says that to get the most enjoyment of thrill-seeking, we have to feel safe and sound in our environment. When our fight-or-flight response kicks in during the deluge of happy chemicals like dopamine, adrenaline, and endorphins, we need to feel that we're protected and secure on the outside.

For example, we enjoy horror movies more because we're getting the excitement in the safe confines of a movie theater. We can get thrilled on roller coasters because (hopefully) our safety harnesses work and the coaster rails are regularly maintained. We experience the trip out of the comfort zone in a safe way. We feel a thrill but ultimately know we won't come to any harm.

The brain also likes novelty, and again that fact is related to dopamine. This chemical is frequently referred to as the "reward chemical" that's part of the brain's "reward center." But according to recent research, dopamine is more associated with our drive to *seek* rewards, rather than just serving as the reward itself. Studies with animals have suggested that the introduction of novelty to an animal's brain also jacks up dopamine levels. The brain then releases dopamine as motivation for the animal to go exploring in search of a reward.

Kent Berridge of the University of Michigan conducted research about displays of pleasure, or "affective reactions" as he calls them, among rodents. His team videotaped rats to gauge how often they exhibited pleasure through sticking out their tongues, licking their paws, or other actions. When dopamine flow was restricted or blocked to the animals' brains, it didn't affect how often they showed those physical pleasure responses. But the dopamine block *did* sap the rats' *motivation*—essentially, they became rodent slackers.

Chasing novelty is, therefore, one potential extension of the act of leaving the comfort zone. There's a certain amount of fear attached, but novelty also delivers actual tangible pleasure. No doubt getting out of the comfort zone is a scary prospect. Even our brains will admit that. But most of the time, the brain physiologically rewards us when we take chances and have new experiences. That positive effect is much stronger than any anxiety.

Jeff Bezos: No Regrets

We see there are benefits in stretching out and taking risks, even as we recognize the process can be terrifying. Conversely, are there any detriments to *not* leaving your comfort zone? This is a drastically different way of thinking that just might force you to take action today.

Jeff Bezos, the founder and CEO of Amazon, once found himself at a crossroads in his life in which he had to make some tough personal resolutions. He came up with a concept he termed the "regret minimization framework." ("Only a nerd would call" it that, Bezos joked.)

The concept of the regret minimization framework is quite basic. Bezos gave himself three very simple mental directives:

1. Project yourself to age 80.

2. Imagine yourself looking back on your life at that age, knowing that you want to feel as few regrets as possible.

3. Ask yourself, "In X number of years, will I regret taking this action (or *not* taking this action)?"

The forward projection to 80 years old and the consideration about what you might regret put a lot of items and issues in very clear perspective. It helps to lessen one's present confusion caused by alternative paths and puts the right decision in clear view. It takes the short-term emotional chatter out of the equation and really forces perspective.

For Bezos, the answer was immediately obvious: if he didn't take the initiative and enter into the information revolution, he'd regret it when he hit age 80. He'd regret not developing his idea for online book sales. He knew he would *not* regret failing, but he would *definitely* regret never giving it a shot.

When Bezos framed his dilemma that way, the decision was almost automatic. He quit his high-paying job at a hedge fund—even walking away from his annual bonus—moved to Seattle, and started running Amazon from his garage. As this writing, Bezos is the wealthiest private citizen in the world, and Amazon is one of the most successful companies in business history.

How do we take Bezos's example into our everyday lives to help us leave the comfort zone? How do we take his framework and use it to assess the pros and cons, the costs and benefits—especially personal costs? And what will we care about in future years that we'll regret *not* doing or trying? What will we miss out on?

The Bezos template is applicable to almost any undertaking, minor or major. Think of something you always tell yourself you "mean to do," and usually can quite easily, but are afraid to make the jump.

You want to start a blog but don't think you're a good enough writer. You want to run the Boston Marathon but don't think you can get in shape. A friend invites you to go skydiving, but the idea scares you to death. But your alleged lack of ability or courage is not the point. The point is this: will you regret never trying it later in life?

Let's take it to a grander, more Bezos-esque scale. Say you have an idea to help build medical facilities in a faraway third world country. The notion appeals to you in terms of potential accomplishment and personal reward, but you're anxious about the reality of being away from home for a year and living in a place where you might not understand the language, culture, or people. Will the potential costs outweigh the personal and emotional benefits—or when you reflect on your life, will you regret never taking that chance?

The regret minimization framework puts our fears under the microscope. It helps us analyze what fears to hold on to and which ones to release. Our fears are usually very minor and diminutive and frequently don't last more than a few seconds. Finally, the framework helps us to examine whether the benefits of a new venture justify the personal price we'll have to shell out.

For many people, breaking out of the comfort zone is natural enough to the extent that it's almost an impulse they can indulge automatically. But for many others, doing so can call up a lot of apprehensions and flat-out fear, even though recesses of our brains crave newness and variety. And for still others, those two natures coexist and rub up against each other. How can we sort out these conflicting mindsets to prepare us for new adventures, challenges, and rewards?

Takeaways:

1. The comfort zone is certainly real, but only as far as you believe in it. That is to say, it is purely mental, and as such, something you can get around.

2. The Yerkes–Dodson curve is a representation of how the comfort zone affects our performance and just why it is so important to step outside and expose yourself to optimal levels of stress. It also demonstrates the importance of pacing yourself and making sure to stay in your comfort zone from time to time for recovery, not rest.

3. The brain likes staying in the comfort zone for the lack of stressors, but we are actually physiologically rewarded for experiencing novelty and thrills. You are happier outside of your comfort zone in the end.

4. The regret minimization framework implores you to ask what you'll regret not doing at the age of 80. This sidesteps perceived obstacles and simply asks what you want to do without regard to your fears or anxieties.

Chapter 2. Comfort-Destroying Mindsets

When I was a teenager, I was in a terrible auto accident. I ran my car into three bus stop benches, two parked cars, a phone booth, a construction crane, and maybe a couple of pedestrians.

Fortunately, I wasn't driving a real car—it was a video simulation in my driver's training class. We sat in these booths with steering wheels and pedals and a TV screen that was supposed to imitate a windshield. We "drove" along with the video we saw, like an arcade game.

Even though it wasn't real, my instructor was no less horrified. I racked up more casualties that morning than anyone he'd ever taught (or so he said). Even as I improved throughout the semester, his words haunted me until the day I had to take my actual, *real* driving test. As I was standing in line with my forms, I could only think about how many cars, benches, lampposts, storefronts, or (heaven forbid) actual people would have to pay the price that afternoon for my getting a legal ID.

Except for missing one right-turn signal, I aced the driving test. My instructor, of course, claimed all the credit with a wink. And everyone survived.

My experience getting my driver's license illustrates a central point in breaking out of the comfort zone. When faced with a new venture outside the comfort zone, one can see it as either a landscape of opportunity or a minefield of trouble. The difference between those perceptions is attitude adjustment, preparing for the situation as it actually is.

The initial key to stretching outside the comfort zone, then, is making a realistic judgment about what you're about to encounter, what traps might (and might not) exist, and how to ready yourself mentally to take it on.

Stop Catastrophizing

Your first step in taking on a new challenge is conquering negative bias about the situation at hand—what we call "catastrophizing."

This mindset is essentially irrational and can persist even if you know it. You discern the situation you're currently being faced with as much worse than it really may be. Left unchecked, this could easily spin off into wild exaggerations of risk and kill off a project before it even gets off the ground. At the least, it can adversely affect you to the point where you take illogical actions or even experience acute anxiety or panic attacks— and you haven't even started yet. In other words, you perceive anything negative to be a catastrophe and anything positive as a catastrophe waiting to happen.

Leaving the comfort zone is only frightening because of what we *fear* might happen. Our imaginations picture all the disastrous ways we'll mess up and the damage that we'll leave in our wake. That's why it's imperative to reel those projections in and see them for the obstructions they are. You might make mistakes, but be realistic about how bad they'll really be—more than likely, you'll realize they were distortions.

Be specific and start small. Perhaps the most typical cognitive mistake that informs catastrophic thinking is overblowing the effect of negative forces. For example, you might assume that because some people feel a certain way, then *everybody* must. Or you might think that if one part of your life is in bad shape, then your entire life is going downhill. Everything is a slippery slope, where something *must* lead to something else. This negativity is our comfort zone's elastic band— it's always pulling us back in, trying to force us to stay inside.

Reading or hearing those fallacies, you'd probably agree that they're not reasonable statements. But even sensible, prudent people can fall into that trap when it comes to their own fears and feelings.

This kind of mindset is related to "all-or-nothing" or "black-and-white" thinking. In this viewpoint, there are only ever two answers to a situation—the polar opposites of "yes/no," "succeed/fail," or "win/lose." It ignores the several gradients and individual factors that could be affecting a situation, many of which might be perfectly fixable or adjustable. Salvaging optimism becomes nearly impossible in this mental environment. You might assume all Italian food uses too much garlic for you to eat or that all romantic comedy movies are too generic for you to enjoy. You could take it in an even more harmful direction: that everyone of a certain ethnic make-up poses some kind of threat to you.

In your initial outlook of a certain scenario, then, be clear and specific about your concerns. Regard them as steps in the program that can be scaled with practical thought and action rather than "deal-breakers" if they're not perfect from the start.

To bring you back to reality, try starting small. Think about your everyday existence: your home, your family, your routines. What qualities about your ordinary, usual life bring you happiness, support, and comfort? What still feels good, makes you feel safe, causes you to laugh, pleases and relaxes you? Remember that these are the things that ground you and will always be constant sources of support. Don't let them be tarnished by thinking in distorted or overgeneralized terms.

Leave the past in the past. Feelings of hopelessness are often the result of fears about the future, both in the short and long term. This is a cognitive flaw in our thinking: we assume that because things are a certain way right now, they'll always be that way forever. Like a person who's been ill for so long they don't think they'll ever recover, we can't imagine what change or improvement will feel like.

This kind of sour thinking is also part of "learned helplessness," when a person believes that if they couldn't exert control over something in their past, then they'll never have control over it again—so it's pointless to even try.

Again, it's easy to fall into this emotional trap, even as we realize how intellectually mistaken it is. Just because something happened once doesn't mean it inevitably will happen again. In fact, it could very well be flat-out *unlikely* to happen again.

So keep a realistic view of the particulars of your situation. Think reasonably about the factors that make up the sum of your action. Instead of automatically classifying something as a surefire flop because of something in the past, try to reframe your feelings into an experience. What did you learn from the past? What would have changed it from a negative to a positive? Instead of dooming yourself at the start, make your knowledge of past errors an *asset* rather than an obstacle. Just keep them in mind when you're venturing outside the comfort zone.

Check the record. Look for information that will help you see how leaving your comfort zone might go. Has what you're about to attempt ever been done by someone else? How did it turn out? Did what you're currently catastrophizing derail their efforts in any way, if it happened at all? Taking a fair, objective look at past history will help you see how your catastrophizing mindset is wrong.

You'll likely find that things have gone fine in your past when attempting something new, and you can also draw on the experiences of other people as a guide.

Something that's new to you is probably not new to *everybody*. It's pretty easy to get information or accounts of people's past adventures to learn what they entailed and how they managed and performed during the event. This is a great way to inject objectivity into your pending event and could obviously make you more legitimately prepared for it.

Now that we know what catastrophizing is, how do we put combatting it into daily practice to help bust out of the comfort zone?

Let's say you're at work and there's a new expense software program you're expected to master within a few weeks. From where you sit at first, it looks daunting and unnecessarily complex. But if you don't learn it, you're afraid that you'll fall behind and become a liability to the organization. You've been historically averse to computers or at least slow to immediately adapt to new tech. Everyone will think you are stupid either way. You'll get fired. People will point and laugh. You're officially anxious.

So start small. Think of how you got to where you are now. You're not going to turn into a liability overnight. Nobody can just waltz in and start doing what you do; you're a unique creature of experience and acumen, and this won't kill your worth in one swoop.

You think you've never been terribly adept at adopting new technology and you don't see that ever changing. But why? This belief is only keeping you in a cycle that feeds into your doubt about yourself. It doesn't have to be a permanent home for your thoughts— once people get over the initial hump of

41

breaking into a program or way of thinking, the hardest part is over. Past experience doesn't dictate future results.

Finally, check with others who can help dispel your fears that something terrible will happen. Should you stumble a bit in learning the new process, people can help out. The ones who built the software fully expect that new users are going to have problems ramping up, so you can check with them. You can also find case studies about how this particular program simplified other companies' work and how it's beneficial.

Assessing and Minimizing Risk

Our inabilities to understand and judge risks outside the comfort zone are what keep us trapped inside it. We don't do a great job of evaluating whether certain hazards are real or unreal.

What we do know is that losing sucks. There's not much argument about that, whether there's a "silver lining" or not. But mixing up loss and failure as permanent conditions, rather than the isolated events they are, can make us risk-averse. As with negative bias, this can prevent us from initiating a project.

A couple of studies have analyzed the mental processes of those who concentrate on avoiding risk. The Columbia Motivation Science Center found that such people are more deliberate and slow about their work. They also emphasize reliability and stability in the products they use or consume, rather than luxury, coolness, or the "*it* factor."

At Harvard University, Francesca Gino and Joshua Margolis further found that those focused on avoiding risk tend to behave in more ethically and honest ways than those who concentrate on promotion. This isn't because those concerned with preventing loss are more principled or upright people; it's because they fear being punished for breaking the rules or stretching out too far.

In short, we are predisposed to avoid risk, just as we're inclined to put it in the spotlight. In doing so, every part of a project becomes circumspect through the lens of potential jeopardy. We're looking for problems—

sometimes *inventing* them where they weren't before so we can avoid the negative consequences of risky behavior. Our inclination to overthink and worry makes us hunt down any reasons we can find to avoid taking action or risk. And with our negativity bias, we overlook all the benefits we could get.

We need to get better at assessing risk because our assessment that risk and danger are truly everywhere is wrong and keeping us in our invisible prisons. That's why it's vital to analyze what is *truly* risky and what's only discerned or sensed as such. In doing so, one needs to ask themselves three questions.

Why is something risky? Get to the core of the issue. Is there substantial real-world evidence that a certain part or process is hazardous or chancy? Or is your worry based on unreal or fraudulent forces, like hearsay, hazy perception, or faint feelings or emotions? Fear often leads to unfounded assumptions that don't reflect fact. Make yourself certain where your trepidation comes from and whether it's sound reasoning or mere panic.

Ask yourself this question three times. Repeating the question, and coming up with more exact answers each time, will help you get closer to what your actual fear or concern might be.

What are the true costs and benefits? What do you really want? What do you stand to gain from the action you want to execute? And what do you stand to lose?

It's again important to be completely sensible about the outcome of your actions. Focus on what constitutes a *true* win or a loss rather than a *perceived* one. Remember that the mind is naturally biased toward the negative—it will inflate the downside and diminish the upside. Make an objective list of pros and cons. If you can't, ask someone who *can* be objective about your venture, especially if they've done it themselves at some point.

What will happen if you do nothing? If you choose not to act, what will come to pass?

Remaining still is often interpreted as minimizing risk—but that's not always true. *Not* taking action could result in a degradation of a situation or circumstance that desperately needed improvement. In those situations, *idleness* is the more acute risk. Again, make a logical evaluation of this scenario, as removed from anxiety or fear (or, for that matter, overly giddy optimism) as you can make it.

Thoughtful risk analysis and abatement is a major part of business—but can we apply it to something more personal? Of course we can.

Just imagine being on the cusp of starting a new relationship but being deathly afraid at the same time. Let's say you've been "out of the game" for a while and the prospect of a new bond at first seems more perilous than it may be.

First, ask why the risk scares you. Again, ask three times to go as far beyond surface level as possible. Are you concerned about something in your partner that you've actually seen from that person—or is it something else that's all your own? Is it based on cross-talk, hearsay, gossip, or overextending your own fears that have kept you behind? Is it based on the common fear of being abandoned or rejected after being emotionally invested?

Then think about what you really want out of this situation and what you fear it will cost you. You want a lasting relationship as a reliable source of security for the rest of your life, but you're afraid you'll lose and miss your independence. You could also be afraid of disappointing the other person in a crippling way. Try to look beyond these projected feelings. Get a clear picture as to what the *real* costs and benefits will be—not just how you feel or fear they'll be. You must differentiate between them to assess risk better.

What will happen if you don't do anything? You might alienate your partner to the point where they just drift off because you're making them wait too long. Or maybe it'll simply remain the same without resulting in any change whatsoever.

Making this decision is an immediate leap out of the comfort zone for, probably, a major segment of the civilized world. After considering all these factors, you might make the decision that's opposite of the one you thought you'd make. But you've gotten yourself to think about it in an honest way, even though it wasn't comfortable to do so. And chances are, you probably feel a lot better about the decision than you would have if you didn't take time to consider it. Each little bit of these questions helps nudge you closer and closer to the exit of the comfort zone.

Letting Go of the Need to Control

One of the most attractive aspects of the comfort zone is how it makes us feel in control. We have better management over our surroundings. The thought of losing control is a terrifying one. We feel that if we're no longer directly navigating a situation, then we'll give up that control and the whole house of cards will come tumbling down.

But one very strong principle of leaving the comfort zone is letting go of that control and our need to have it.

Amy Arnsten of the Yale School of Medicine conducted studies on certain effects of the prefrontal cortex. This part of the brain is generally concerned with regulating our behavior, personality, impulse, and focus ability. One of her findings was that the brain *really* depends on a sense of control.

"The loss of prefrontal function only occurs when we feel out of control," Arnsten said. "It's the prefrontal cortex itself that is determining if we are in control or not. Even if we have the illusion that we are in control, our cognitive functions are preserved."

The prefrontal cortex is basically our repository of conscious thoughts. When its sense of control is disrupted or lost, then we revert to other, more agitated parts of the limbic system like the amygdala, which is *all* emotion. That could trigger our fight-or-flight instincts, with massive quantities of adrenaline or cortisol unleashing loads of fear and stress.

So obviously, we're conditioned to believe that control equals security. When we're in control of a situation we feel safe. We're in the driver's seat, nothing will escape our attention, and we've got everything handled. What could *possibly* go wrong?

Control also indicates *certainty*. This is one of the most common opinions about control. Humans crave certainty more than nearly anything else. Knowing what will happen in the future keeps us from worrying about it. In fact, the thirst for control often springs from our wish to be able to predict the future. We try to envision the worst-case scenario and plan around it.

New experiences, though, are *always* out of our control. You can't dictate the terms of a new experience because you don't even know what you're in for yet. Change is not only inevitable; it's frequently quick and impossible to foretell. After we embrace that truth, we start loosening our grip on the aspects of life we try to keep under command.

Desiring control and not having it leads to worry and unrest. Irrationality sets in, and we're back to thinking about all the adverse things that can occur again. The more we crave control, the more we live out of a sense of dread and distress—and the less we'll experience.

So how can you slacken your clutches over a situation? As with everything else in this chapter, it's a matter of corrective thinking.

***Is it that you* can't *let go of control—or you* won't?** This is probably the most important question. Is your having control really a requirement in this process, or is it merely just a reinforcement of your will?

Ask yourself what you're really afraid of when you lose your control. It might follow that your control is not absolutely necessary—it may just be an instinct or impulse you've always had but never scrutinized.

The unknown is always scary. This always has been and always will be the case. But "scary" is not negative.

There will always be apprehension when we're about to chart unknown waters. It's how we view that apprehension—positive or negative—that affects our achievement. Scary isn't negative.

But at its heart, the unknown is merely a set of circumstances, at least part of which we can expect through considered thinking. In most everyday situations, the fear of an unknown overwhelms the very possible reality that it won't be that drastic of a change.

In truth, the unknown stops being scary precisely at the point where it becomes known. So the unknown is not the same as fear. If you can transform that fear into a logical plan or set of steps to adjust to whatever comes, the unknown becomes a simple problem with a *solution*. Rather than focusing on the scary parts, look past them to what answers they'll provide—and what you can do about them.

Understand what you* don't *control. Namely, anything outside your own efforts. In almost any course of action more complicated than switching on a light—that is to say, pretty much everything else—there's a series of x-factors, events and details that would happen whether you're there or not. You can't control those aspects at all—therefore, it's counterproductive to worry about them. That's just making yourself suffer twice if misfortune occurs (and *still* suffering once if things turn out well).

There's a difference between being alert and being worried. If a worry helps you make good decisions and preparations, then that's fine. But after a certain point, worry becomes a hindrance—an additional barrier that sits alongside all the other barriers you originally worried about.

To put all this together in a practical example, let's say you're planning a cross-country road trip after years of not having a real vacation.

But you're wary about going. You haven't maintained your car as well as you could have. You're not certain of how you'll react with other people away from your hometown, and although you're anxious to travel, you're a little afraid of just getting up and leaving.

First, ask whether your will is the only thing making you feel you need to control the situation. Maybe you're afraid of getting lost—even though you're not tied to a certain set of instructions. You've always admired those who struck out on their own with no roadmap in mind, but you might have thought that they were being irresponsible. In that case, it's more that you won't let go of control.

The benefits of traveling to unfamiliar places are well-known—they expand your frame of reference and open you up to possibilities that you simply don't have at home. As far as what you can and can't control—well, you can get your car repaired, at least to the point where it's travel-ready. Or you could take another means of transportation. Beyond that, there are several factors you can't control: the immediate actions of strangers, weather or road conditions, and what will happen at home when you're away from it. Take care of what you can and don't worry about what you can't.

Play, Exploration, and Curiosity

There was a point in all of our lives when we had no control, no mental restrictions, and no catastrophic fears, and we had *nothing* but the unknown in front of us. Virtually everything we experienced was completely new, and we went out of our comfort zones without giving it another thought. We didn't even know what a comfort zone *was* to begin with because we perceived very little danger.

This was, of course, when we were children. During our youth, almost all of us dealt with the unknown by asking about it, investigating it, and—most importantly—*playing* with it.

At some point afterward, we may have decided that approaching new things with a sense of "play" wasn't appropriate anymore. But *why?* Our curiosity isn't meant to age or get outdated—it's still the same as it was when we were kids.

By following where your curiosity leads, indulging in the same pleasure you had when you were a child at play, getting out of your comfort zone becomes considerably easier. Distracting yourself with these new sensations and activities will keep you away from fear and nervousness. Not only will it break you out of your comfort zone, but it'll make you forget what zone you're inhabiting in the first place. Exploration and curiosity will make it so your comfort zone doesn't even have a definition at all. They can remove your boundaries and limits that easily.

If you've ever wondered about something, or how that something worked, there's nothing stopping you from learning about it. Pursue that answer, no matter where you're led. The positive motivators that spur you to chase your interests will always be stronger than negative motivators.

That road also leads you to learn new skills, challenge your ideas, and try new activities in the name of satisfying your curiosity. You'll envision the world as one of possibilities and new exploits—instead of a minefield.

So find what fascinates you. It might not show up at your front door; you might have to go looking for it. You might have to sift through trash that doesn't interest you in the slightest. But the very process of exploration itself will always result in some surprises—which, you guessed it, will rev up your curiosity again. Your mind may not even be *able* to close up after that.

There are so many situations this attitude supports in a positive way that it's almost better to ask when it *doesn't* help. If you're taking an online course in coding, playing around with the commands and structure can open up new ideas. You could try cooking in an extremely exotic cuisine you've never tried before and mess around with the ingredients to see how it affects the taste. If you're making a public presentation, you can try to inject humor, storytelling, or other playfulness to make it more interesting (and therefore drive home your point). All of these methods help you regain your natural, childlike sense of wonder and possibly open up avenues to new experiences and beliefs.

Fear, risk, loss of control, and restriction are all impediments—that is to say, expected elements—of any new and unfamiliar situation. While it's natural to experience and expect them on the course outside your comfort zone, handling them in the early stages will bring you more successful conquests over what still holds many adults back. Even if your efforts don't result in 100% success, they'll likely be successful enough—and you'll have learned much more for the next time.

Takeaways:

1. Breaking the comfort zone begins with the mindsets you have about leaving it in the first place. The first mindset to overcome is that of catastrophizing—the feeling that everything is falling apart at any moment. This is driven by a skewed and fearful approach.

2. The next mindset is to assess risk better and more accurately. We stay in the comfort zone because we feel everything is too risky. Similar to catastrophizing, this makes us prone to inaction. We assess risk emotionally when it should be placed in more grounded terms.

3. We don't leave the comfort zone because we feel a need to be in control of what happens to us. Of course, anything new or novel is inherently outside of our control because we don't know it. Our mindsets must become more comfortable with change, novelty, and a lack of control over everything.

4. What would your seven-year old self want to do? They were fearless, without filter, and gave no regard as to potential risks or fears. This is whom you might want to channel more frequently.

Chapter 3. Breaking Your Beliefs

Leaving one's comfort zone is a willful act of breaking away from a sense of safety. You might perceive yourself as being too weak or frightened to escape your comfort zone, but the reality is different.

You're not too weak or frightened.

Excuses are what keep your fears and flaws alive. They're standalone, limiting beliefs that you may hold on to because they feel reliable. But what they really do is generate self-fulfilling prophecies, one after another, holding back your potential in the process.

In this chapter, we learn how to identify what parts of our belief systems are actual truths and what are misconceptions we've allowed to take root.

Types of Courage

"Courage" is a word that we usually associate with giant achievements that don't happen every day. But there are several kinds of courage, and understanding this fact within the context of our beliefs makes it easier to move outside the comfort zone. You probably possess or embody at least two of the types that follow below.

We speak of courage to describe unusual instances of heroism that don't happen all the time: firefighters who walk into burning buildings, soldiers in battle, or protestors standing up against injustice. But we rely on subtler, maybe less glorious types of courage practically every day. Author Steven Kotler identified various types of courage that don't necessarily fall into our traditional idea of bravery or daring but are as powerful and real as the fortitude we know from folk tales and history books.

Some of Kotler's types of courage include the following:

Physical courage. This is easily identifiable, Kotler says, as "the willingness to push the limits of one's body." Athletic competition is the clearest example of physical courage, but Kotler also identifies individual sports or activities that incorporate the risk of injury.

Battle fortitude. This refers to the shared will of a group of united soldiers—whether in actual war or athletic competition—where the risk is shared with other teammates. Kotler notes that it's more of a psychological strategy than an "individual necessity."

Moral courage. Kotler likens this type of courage with the protests of Mahatma Gandhi and Rosa Parks: "the courage to stand up for one's beliefs in the face of overwhelming opposition." This could be exemplified in participation in protests or a simple letter to an editor.

Intellectual courage. The bravery to stand up for ideas, opinions, or emotional realities that might go against the grain or the tide of popular opinion. It can be something of a double-edged sword, however—arguing in favor of civil rights for marginalized people carries a certain weight that's absent in arguments for, say, the idea that the world is flat.

Empathetic courage. Kotler says this "should probably be the most celebrated of all categories." As the name defines, it's the courage to develop deep sentiment or compassion for other beings. Kotler cites the animal rescue community as a good example.

Parental courage. An extension of parental instinct, this is exemplified as the drive to rescue or protect children from adverse situations or disasters: jumping into a pool to save a drowning child or Kotler's example of a parent rushing into a burning building to save their offspring.

Decision-making in the face of uncertainty. As I write this in late 2017, this may be the most precarious social environment for decisions in our lifetimes. "The proliferation of choice is expanding exponentially and psychologically crippling," Kotler says. Our choices in everything from political candidates to where we buy clothes, previously merely harmless options, are now underscored with epic doubt.

Emotional courage. Maybe the most difficult type of courage that doesn't involve direct physical peril, emotional bravery means making a difficult personal decision—most obviously a break-up or divorce—that virtually ensures a prolonged period of misery for the decider. "You're still willing to suffer those consequences for a greater emotional payoff later," Kotler explains.

Tactical courage. Similar to battle fortitude, tactical courage is a bit thornier because it involves decisions that puts *others'* lives at risk—like a president deciding to declare war or a field operative being sent into a dangerous foreign conflict.

Fiscal courage. Colloquially stated, "putting your money where your mouth is." This attitude happens when you put your cash, livelihood, or currency of survival at risk. "Money is nothing beyond a stand-in for all things survival," Kotler says. The act could range from investing in volatile stocks to ponying up cash for a fantasy football league.

Not all of these forms of courage are easy to manage, and as we've seen, some (intellectual or fiscal courage especially) might not be perfect indicators of valor. But the point is that courage takes many forms. Even if we don't see ourselves as disciplined pillars of strength or resiliency, chances are we rely on these small forms of courage much more often than we think. And all of them can help us break out of the comfort zone.

The Spotlight Effect

Well, you've done it now. You wrote a blog post last night. You might have had a bit to drink, and that might have enabled you. What's more, you wrote about an opinion of yours that's sure to cause a lot of controversy:

you adamantly insist that *Friends* was a better TV show than *Seinfeld*. You lay out your case in explicit, very confrontational detail. Then you go to sleep.

You wake up the next morning, fully rested, but with this terrible sinking feeling. You happen to know for a fact that your boss at work owns DVDs for every single season of *Seinfeld*. He's bragged about it. He quotes lines from the show. Sometimes he delivers anecdotes based on the show. He classifies everyone he meets as a Jerry, George, Elaine, or Kramer. Everyone at your company knows about this.

And now you regret your post last night. Surely your boss is going to read about this opinion of yours. So will everyone you work with. And their *families* might read your opinion, too. You think you might know someone whose cousin actually worked on the show or something. What if *he* sees it? Then it'll be just a matter of time before Jerry Seinfeld himself calls you because he can't believe what he's seeing. "How *could* you!"

he'll ask. "It's as if I wore that puffy shirt all for naught!"

You can't take any of those chances happening, so you zip out of bed and delete the blog post. Whatever damage you have already done to your reputation is past, and all you can do now is contain the fallout. It's probably too late to salvage your rep with your boss or coworkers, though.

You go to work that day, and it's weird. Everyone's acting as if nothing happened. Even your boss. In fact, your boss asks if you want some coffee, since he's going to get some for himself anyway. These are not the actions of a man whose personal tastes you had ripped to shreds mere hours before. Is he just setting you up to punish you later?

What you do not yet realize is that nobody actually saw that blog post. Not your boss, not your coworkers, not their families, not even Jerry Seinfeld. Turns out most of them didn't even know you *have* a blog.

We often don't act out in certain manners because we're afraid what the reaction from others will be. We hold ourselves back from bold moves from fear of judgment, rejection, or derision from others who'll deem us as stupid or worthy of scorn.

The biggest reason for this reaction is the spotlight effect. It's the misconception that we are the focus of other people's attention. Everyone is watching every move, hearing every utterance, or reading every word we make. Therefore, we need to be careful, which makes getting outside the comfort zone much more difficult.

It's best explained by issuing a challenge. Think of the last two or three embarrassing things that you did. Whether it was spilling something on your clothes, making an awkward body sound in public, or getting into a drunken rant at a bar. However major or minor the embarrassments were, ponder them for a minute. This should be fairly easy to do.

Then, think of the last two or three embarrassing things you saw *someone else* do or the last couple of times you witnessed someone else behaving boorishly, having a physically awkward moment, or getting into their *own* drunken rants at a bar. *This* exercise isn't so easy at all. Unless you were somehow a *part* of how this person got embarrassed, chances are it will be quite hard.

This is the spotlight effect. We imagine that, since we're the lead character in our own walking movies, that attention is always trained on us. We think we're walking around with an ever-present spotlight and people are always noticing, thinking, or talking about our every move and whisper. If you're not a raging narcissist, the only effects are that it can make one very paranoid.

But here's the truth: no one really cares that much. They don't care about what you do or say. They don't remember 99% of the foolish things you've done. Nobody talks about you all the time. In fact, nobody even thinks about you that frequently unless they're your best friend, your partner, or your conjoined twin.

It's very easy to understand how the spotlight effect happens, because we all feel it. You're the center of your own world because you happen to be *you*. Without you, you don't exist. That is probably the most absurdly obvious statement in this book. But it's meant to explain how outsized your own significance actually is—your importance *apart* from your own life is largely an illusion.

Furthermore, nobody else is stuck with you or hinging on your every move and statement because—you guessed it—they're consumed with their *own* spotlight effect! They're worrying too much about the lead character in *their* lives, themselves, to be microscopically involved with yours, judging your every move.

Just a few years ago the spotlight effect might have been a little more innocuous—but social media has changed all that. When we're on Facebook, Twitter, Snapchat, Instagram, or any other service, we're not just people that others know: we're now media companies. Very *small* media companies, true, but we do the same things. We publish words, we report news (fake or otherwise), we distribute videos and music, and we establish and commodify our own personalities. All that makes it even *easier* to imagine the spotlight effect taking hold in a whole new way.

Most of us don't know about the spotlight effect. Even if we are aware of such egotism, we don't necessarily consider it an affliction. Either way, people spend their days consumed with what the rest of the world is thinking about them, without once coming to the realization that nobody is.

But what if you acknowledge the spotlight effect is merely just that—an *effect*? A *Matrix*-like half-reality that only exists as your own invention? If you realize that nobody's really thinking about you all that much, you're all set up to feel legitimate liberation.

You're not so afraid to speak your mind if you feel like people aren't focusing on you. You don't get sidetracked or mortified at the clumsy mistakes you make every once in a while. You'll stop fixating about how your online persona appears to others.

In short, you're not thinking about other people that much, which is great because they're not thinking about you. I repeat: that's a *good* thing. It gives you the freedom to move around and do whatever you want, all the while secure in the notion that nobody gives a rip. If they do, they'll forget about it in a couple of minutes when they've found another mistake somebody else made.

The fruits of this exercise can also strengthen the *real* bonds you have with close friends and family, because in most cases, not only are your perceived fouls and mess-ups not a big deal to them, but they've seen you be that way several times and they're still around. They might even love you *because* you make those mistakes. When you find yourself in a group where you're talking freely, where there's no fear of reprisal or judgment for simple errors or mistakes, when you're just being yourself—well, at least for a while, you've beaten the spotlight effect.

Internal Demons

Judgment from others isn't all we fear in making new choices outside the comfort zone. Our own psyches and emotions give us plenty of self-generated misgivings as well. To break outside the comfort zone, we also have to negotiate with our own internal demons, and those suckers can be tricky.

The first rank of internal demons are our defense mechanisms: the lies we tell ourselves. They're especially troublesome because we might not even realize they're lies.

The term "defense mechanisms" was first coined in the setting of psychoanalytic therapy. Over time, it became so recognized and prevalent that it's part of our common, daily language. That fact alone tells you how familiar they are.

Defense mechanisms are called into being as unconscious, psychological reactions that rationalize or ease our anxiety. They protect us from the unpleasantness of confronting our weakness and foibles. They guard us from having to deal with threats, challenges, or anything else we don't want to think about— in other words, anything outside the comfort zone. They make us feel better ourselves.

Think of the last time you said somebody was "in denial" about a certain matter or when you last accused somebody of "rationalizing." You were referring to their use of defense mechanisms—and apparently, not a very successful use of them since you expressed that opinion.

Modern psychoanalysis, as you may know, is a direct descendant of the work of Austrian psychologist Sigmund Freud. He developed a well-known model of personality that depicts the nature of the defense mechanism in great detail.

In Freud's model, the aspect of our personality that interacts with reality is the *ego*. This definition isn't to be confused with the one that describes the level of someone's self-esteem or arrogance. Freud's ego is simply the part of our being that has to arbitrate between our conscious and subconscious forces and keep them in balance so we can live our lives in productive ways (or, at very least, be presentable in public).

The forces the ego has to contend with are the *id* and the *superego*. They are not so much opposing forces as they are partners who have very different methods. Well, *extremely* different methods.

The id's main goal is to get everything. It wants to fulfill all the desires, needs, and impulses a person might have. It's a feral, primal part of our personalities that has no regard for social decorum, appropriateness, morality, or even our intellectual opinions on what we want or need. It's basically a savage animal.

The superego, on the other hand, is driven by our moral codes and ideals. It houses all the values we acquired from various sources: parents, churches, other family members, and what society generally approves of as being the proper way to go about our business. It's not as fun as the id, for sure. But it answers to our notions of right and wrong.

Freud believed that the ego constructs defense mechanisms to shield itself from the wild brawls the id and superego often have.

These conflicts are virtual breeding grounds for anxiety and guilt, and the ego tries to head off those distasteful feelings by calling upon us to, essentially, lie to ourselves about what we're feeling.

It's important to know what is true and what is a product of a defense mechanism. And it's difficult because they're often easy to see when *other* people use them—but not so much when we're using them ourselves, which makes it harder for us to get outside the comfort zone.

There are many ways to execute our defense mechanism that will seal us inside the comfort zone. These three are among the most common:

Rationalization. Finding excuses or plausible explanations for bad feelings or acts is a common way to deflect blame or guilt we might have. They can also keep us chained to the comfort zone.

You decide against going roller-skating because "that's something only kids do." You don't take a trip on an airplane because "their service is terrible . . . and what's keeping that big hunk of metal up in the sky anyway? It could crash any moment." You decide not to volunteer at a food bank because "it's not a real solution to the problem of poverty anyway, so what's the point?"

All those responses are rationalizations. We provide ourselves with several excuses and distort the facts to explain our desired course of action.

Many people with sensitive egos are so at ease with making excuses that they might not even be truly aware they're doing so. Many of us, in fact, are quite prepared to believe the lies we tell ourselves.

As a defense mechanism, rationalization is somewhat like intellectualization (below), but it deals with your own bad behavior to buffer you against negative or painful emotions. People rationalize to shore up their insecurities or remorse. After committing a regretful action, they try to make their feelings more neutral by writing it off as an "oops" moment—or finding elaborate ways to skip the blame to someone else.

It's always easier when there's someone else to take the heat for our own actions, especially if they're embarrassing or shameful. If you get angry and lose your temper in front of people whose acceptance you want, you might attribute your outburst to a situation that was outside your control. You could even contort the situation to the point of blaming someone else for *provoking* your reaction.

The desired endgame in rationalization is acquittal of your own desires and intentions and the conviction of someone else's malicious purposes (or at least the inherent corruption of society at large). You may know better, but at least you *think* nobody else does.

Denial. Your neighbor's dog is a pest and a half. It's always coming into your yard and ransacking your garbage can and depositing his waste in prime places on your lawn. You really mean to talk to your neighbor about keeping his dog under control. But you don't like confrontations. You avoid them if you can. They're way out of your comfort zone.

So you tell yourself it's no big deal. "When you get down to it, there's really no problem. The dog's not hurting anything. Besides, animals are supposed to roam free." The issue, though, is that you don't want to take a chance and state your case to your neighbor. You tell yourself the threat doesn't exist, which makes it acceptable for the dog to decorate your lawn. The problem never comes up.

This is an example of denial. It involves blocking external events from awareness. It's comprised of refusal to experience a situation when it becomes too much to handle.

Denial is a dangerous and primitive defense. Nobody disregards reality and gets away with it for very long. Sometimes you need to face as much truth as you can to deal with an adverse predicament—but not even acknowledging that truth, or actively evading it, can make it multiple times worse than the discomfort you're feeling now.

For example, smokers might refuse to admit to themselves that cigarettes are bad for their health. By using denial, you simply refuse to accept that reality. Denial could also get an assist from rationalization: "Well, I'm just a social smoker."

This can be applied to any bad habit or practice that one wants to distance themselves from, like excessive substance abuse, compulsive shopping, or gambling. But in a weird twist, admonishing one to stay away from those activities—"just say no"— without investigating how they work is *another* form of denial. It mollifies the superego but doesn't solve the problem.

Denial might also be used by victims of trauma or disasters. In some of those cases, it must be said, denial might be at least temporarily necessary as an initial protective response. But in the long run, denial can prevent you from understanding information about yourself and your life that you seriously need to address. The consequences of that thinking can be destructive.

Intellectualization. This form of defense mechanism is, perhaps, the most misunderstood. That's ironic, of course, because the aim of intellectualization can be described as an effort to understand *too much*.

Say you're choosing classes for college. You're pretty good with literature, history, social studies, anything connected with the liberal arts. But you need a math component as well. You just don't do math. Numbers, for whatever reason, frighten you. They're a challenge for you to deal with.

So instead of signing up for algebra class, you give explanations why you don't have to take it. "How does anybody use algebra in everyday life? Where do you see those equations in the world, apart from a blackboard? That's why we have calculators. It's a pointless pursuit. There is no real-world application for algebra."

You've talked yourself into feeling okay about your desired course of action. Intellectualization seeks to find a convoluted yet logical explanation for whatever course of action you want. It's a way to reduce anxiety or head off anguish by thinking about events from a cold, clinical perspective and saying "Yes . . . my explanation does make sense . . . therefore, it is okay!"

Truth be told, sometimes intellectualization is necessary to complete certain tasks that might be hard to get through emotionally, for whatever reason. But more often, it is used as a tool to feel okay with what you want to do. Funnily enough, the smarter you are, the more likely you are to use intellectualization because it involves creating narratives and connecting small dots.

I say intellectualization is "misunderstood" because few of us would ever think that logically looking at a situation could ever be bad. But it's a matter of *why* you're really making that effort. Using the intellectual process to buffer against our more unpleasant feelings is, in the long run, an ineffective tactic.

The mind and heart are supposed to be collaborators in our lives, and employing the brain to shout down the spirit is, to be simplistic, using the organ in the wrong way. When this process keeps us from enjoying challenges or new adventures, then it's keeping us confined to the comfort zone.

Unspoken, Limiting Beliefs

The comfort zone is lined with what's familiar to us—not just what feels good, but what feels "right." Our decisions about what is right are formed by our beliefs—the mental notions and assumptions we have about ourselves and the world around us. We adhere to them as absolute, incontrovertible truths. Frequently they spring from emotions and psychological sources (and can also be irrational). They're shaped through our experiences and interactions with the world. They comprise our mental model.

Quite often, our beliefs may be right. They may dictate the best pathway for a solution or a statement of intent. But they can also hold us back. They can serve as a hindrance in the pursuit of our dreams and the actualization of our potential.

Many of them accumulated and formed when we were children. We learned them through interactions with others and reinforced them through our parents' and authorities' discipline—for example, when we were scolded for doing something wrong or in a way our parents didn't expect us to.

Negative beliefs feed into our lack of self-worth as children, and we reap those seeds when we become adults. They convince us, almost without us asking, that we're not capable, not talented enough, or just flat-out stupid.

These beliefs are locking you in your comfort zone. They tell you everything outside that zone is dangerous and scary. And they'll serve as internal neon signs that flash in your head if you even entertain the idea of stretching out: "I'm not smart," "I'm not good enough,"

"I'm too ugly," "I can't do it," "I don't deserve it." Therefore, you don't take action.

Some of these beliefs stem from the pain-and-pleasure response. When you come across a specific situation, your brain asks whether making a certain decision or taking a specific action will result in pain or pleasure. Your decision to act is made to help you avoid pain or gain pleasure. (Even if you choose to do a physically painful thing, you might be doing it because it makes you happy, although it certainly won't help you convince someone to sell you life insurance.)

This decision provides insight about the hidden belief at the core of that particular psychological rule. Your experience with past pain and pleasure backs up and informs those beliefs. For example, as a child, other children may have teased you about being physically clumsy. Twenty years later, you back out of an invitation to taking dancing classes because you think you're not physically suited to dance. You avoid reawakening that ridicule—the pain—but you also lose out on learning a new thing. Therefore, your current fear of leaving the comfort zone is because it's been reinforced through past pain or pleasure.

Other beliefs are generalizations you make about things, people, and life. These beliefs are very easy to hold on to because they cushion our constructs about the world and might even make us feel temporarily superior. But in addition to being unfair to the subjects being generalized, they could keep your own adventurousness in check because they paint the picture of a world that isn't meant for you or available to you.

For example, let's say you have two friends who were from opposite sides of the United States. One grew up in rural California and the other grew up in New York City. You grew up in the rural area, so you think you know the people pretty well. You've also formed a rather harsh conclusion about people from New York—you think they're a bit arrogant, pushy, and sharp-edged. Maybe you got that way by hearing your parents dismiss New Yorkers as being "too big for their britches." Or you saw a couple of movies set in New

York that presented all of its population in a disparaging light.

Whatever the reason, you have transported this opinion into a belief about *all* New Yorkers. And you accept the entirety of your farm friend because you believe people from your hometown, or at least not from New York, are more reliable or better company.

In reality, New Yorkers are all different, many of them good-hearted. And not everyone with a rural background has a spotless constitution. But you've formed a generalization about New York based on information that's patchy at best. It affects your treatment of the New Yorker in some way—even if, outwardly, you try to be nice to them. Spelled out: you move to New York and have zero friends because you have limiting beliefs about them, which make you not take action

The solution to limiting beliefs is to realize many of them can be easily disproven with evidence to the contrary. They can also be clarified by "alternative explanations." These aren't the same as evidence, which is concrete proof. Rather, alternative explanations are essentially made-up reinterpretations of actual evidence. They shape the meaning of the evidence to fit whatever point we're trying to make.

In our example, your belief can be countered if your New York friend turns out to be generous and empathetic—evidence to the contrary. Or that friend could talk about *why* New Yorkers can sometimes be perceived as mean: it's an insanely busy city 24 hours a day and the competition to survive is rougher than in other places. That is an alternative explanation.

Well-developed and thoughtful beliefs are good things to have. They remind us what we stand for and help us navigate our daily lives. But it's harder to admit that some of our inbred beliefs could be restricting us to the confines of the comfort zone—doing so would be an admission that some of our beliefs might be wrong.

Just remember, the brain is a malleable entity when it comes to belief systems. It can be hard to crack through the most stubborn beliefs that keep us down because we use them as safety devices. But with self-inquiry, earnestness, and being as open as possible, those confining beliefs can be dismantled, one by one.

Takeaways:

1. If you want to leave the comfort zone, you must first believe that you can indeed do it. The first way to instill that belief is to understand how many different types of courage exist and how many you might exhibit that aren't the traditional ones you can fixate on. You can leave the comfort zone; you just have to find your own avenue to do it.

2. The spotlight effect can be crippling. If we imagine that every one of our actions is dissected under a microscope, we might never do anything. But it's also a cognitive malfunction that is almost always incorrect.

3. Defense mechanisms are some of the nastiest barriers to leaving the comfort zone because they act to protect your ego. To protect your ego, you don't attempt to do anything you have a chance in failing at. The most common defense mechanisms are rationalization, denial, and intellectualization.

4. Aside from defense mechanisms, we might have beliefs about ourselves or the world that have been ingrained in us since childhood. They are largely unconscious until you examine the deep bases for your opinions and beliefs. They usually don't hold up under evidence or scrutiny.

Chapter 4. Run Before You're Ready

Getting started is the most difficult part of any process. There's *never* a perfect time to start anything new or scary. Something is *always* being interrupted, and you will *always* have to experience growing pains. Except for the most feverishly task-oriented people, beginning something unfamiliar is determinedly outside the comfort zone. It's common for us to procrastinate in such situations, either to prepare as much as possible—what we call "analysis paralysis"—or avoid kickoff until there's no alternative but to launch.

But too much resistance to start a new effort, even in the name of "preparation," creates a sort of vacuum no matter what the intent. Dale Carnegie made this point when he said, "Inaction breeds doubt and fear. Action breeds confidence and courage. If you want to conquer fear, do not sit home and think about it. Go out and get busy."

To get moving, you have to get into the habit of acting a tiny bit prematurely, before you feel ready. This chapter is about encouraging action: "leap first, look second." It might not always be the best course of action for every new venture you take up, but it's great for leaving the comfort zone.

Perfectionism as Procrastination

Everyone agrees that procrastination is a bad thing. But striving to always be perfect is a noble and good pursuit, right?

Well, not so fast.

Both procrastination and perfectionism are fraught with difficulty. They also tend to happen together to form an infinite loop that can sap your productivity and your psyche. Procrastination has a simple definition: delaying commencement of a project until the last possible moment. Perfectionism is the natural extension and also holds up our actions and keeps us stagnant.

Perfectionism is sometimes called "the highest form of self-abuse." Striving for perfection is unreasonable almost by definition because it doesn't even exist. Since perfection is almost never necessary in most situations—unless you're a brain surgeon—it's nothing more than an attempt to preserve one's own self-worth. More often than not, it hinges on the expectations of others.

The concern that we must carry out all of our activities as seamlessly and blemish-free as we can—or we don't do it at all—keeps us from venturing outside of our comfort zone. It keeps us from taking a chance with half-formed ideas or working without a net and forces us to stay where it's safe and convenient and where nobody offers any criticism.

Procrastination is a *symptom* of perfectionism. Since perfectionists fear not completing their tasks perfectly, they simply put it off for as long as they can. They feel that not meeting their prescribed goals means there's something bad, wrong, or unworthy about them. They fear that failure will involve criticism or ridicule from either internal or external voices. The acuter that fear gets, the longer perfectionists procrastinate.

One thing that should be made clear is that procrastination and laziness aren't the same thing. Indeed, if there's anything giving procrastinators any fuel, paradoxically, it's their burning desire to work *well*. They have a low tolerance for frustration and failure—but for them, procrastination has become the activity through which they channel those anxieties. When they feel the standards are sky-high and perceive accomplishment to be outside their capabilities, they sidestep the discomfort through diversion.

Besides, you already know that perfection is almost never achievable in any endeavor. You know that nobody's perfect, no project is perfect, and nothing ever goes 100% perfectly in any situation. So calling yourself a "perfectionist" is just an excuse: you think it's not possible, so you don't even start. You're not a perfectionist with exacting standards; you're just insulating yourself from discomfort and change.

Perfectionism is also wrapped up in what we *believe* other people's expectations of us are. This desire for external approval can lead us toward inactivity because if we're not doing anything, then nobody can see us fail. But just like the spotlight effect in the last chapter, you have to remember the most likely truth: nobody's watching, nobody cares, and nobody else matters, primarily because they're so wrapped up with themselves that they won't notice mistakes you might make. Let your desire to impress others go and try to decouple your performance from your sense of self-worth.

Furthermore, realize there's a crucial difference between perfection and excellence. Striving for excellence is a normal, healthy drive based on performing at your best. In stark contrast, perfectionism is a negative emotion working from a fear of mistakes or insufficiency. Excellence is independent of that.

Remember that perfectionism is an unrealistic, unobtainable thing—it can only keep you from acting upon something and give you excuses not to act. It's something keeping you squarely in the comfort zone, because it has deceived you.

Planning Paralysis

Another friend of the comfort zone is endless rumination—analyzing, assessing, inventing, predicting, and otherwise appraising potential actions rather than actually getting up and *doing* the thing. A lot of companies, including some of the most successful in the world, sometimes find themselves wrangling over "meeting culture." This is where multiple, fact-finding conferences are scheduled, often one right after the other. There are jump-off meetings, weekly staff meetings, department meetings, and personal one-on-one meetings. Sometimes scheduled meetings are nothing more than checkpoints to find out how a certain project is progressing. Well, the project *would* be progressing quite nicely if you didn't have to attend all these meetings.

You have to have occasional meetings, of course. But in the end, they're simply an abstraction of work, not the actual execution of work—meaning, simply, there's a lot of planning going on at these conferences and nobody actually picking up the actual shovel, so to speak.

This notion is parallel to what we call "planning paralysis"—when planning becomes a higher priority than actually *doing* something. The job of *planning* to leave your comfort zone takes precedence over, or at least valuable time from, your actual project.

Ultimately, it's another form of procrastination. Gathering more information than you absolutely need, conducting multiple analyses of different ways to achieve something, combing over minute and usually unnecessary details, debating back and forth in your own head about multiple scenarios—

all of these actions are used as something that will postpone your taking action. After all, it's easier to plan than do.

Planning in itself is a kind of comfort zone, not just because you can do it from a couch. To do something, you have to get outside and risk a certain vulnerability. So it's always easier to keep planning, because technically it's useful to your task. You can lead yourself to believe you're being productive toward your overall goal.

For example, you can spend hours in a recliner leafing through cooking websites to find better ways of making a particular dish. You might find a perfectly decent recipe but then see another one that might be more interesting. You can keep on looking up additional recipes and maybe even stumble upon a side dish you'd like to make as well. You find a lot of possibilities, and they all look fairly good. Next thing you know, it's five minutes before dinnertime and you haven't so much as filled a pot with water. And on top of it all, the very first recipe you looked at may have been more than sufficient.

Planning to map out precision and sewing up random details isn't the worst way to go about projects. But more likely, planning is a device that helps one avoid action to mollify our fears and anxieties. When we're spinning our wheels, it's because we've started listening to that inner voice that likes to harangue us into believing all we do will fail and we're foolish for trying.

You won't necessarily be ready when you've finished planning either. The end of a meeting doesn't automatically flip the light switch. Leave open the possibility that you'll never feel truly ready, even after you've laid out your plans. When you realize that, it might spur you to take off the thinking cap, put on some overalls, and start digging in. But keep in mind that over-planning is an often redundant process that people hide behind, never to leave the comfort zone.

The 40–70 Rule

Many of us are reluctant to take actions outside the comfort zone unless we have all the pertinent information we need about them. But can you actually have *too* much information to start something new?

Former U.S. Secretary of State Colin Powell has a rule of thumb about making decisions and coming to a point of action. He says that any time you face a hard choice, you should have *no less* than 40% and *no more* than 70% of the information you need to make that decision. In that range, you have enough information to make an informed choice but not so much intelligence that you lose your resolve and simply stay abreast of the situation.

If you have less than 40% of the information you need, you're essentially shooting from the hip. You don't know quite enough to move forward and will probably make a lot of mistakes. Conversely, if you chase down more data until you get more than 70% of what you need (and it's unlikely that you'll truly need anything above this level), you could get overwhelmed and uncertain. The opportunity may have passed you by and someone else may have beaten you by starting already.

But in that sweet spot between 40% and 70%, you have enough to go on and let your intuition guide your decisions. In the context of Colin Powell, this is where effective leaders are made: the ones who have instincts that point in the right direction are who will lead their organization to success.

For our purposes of breaking out of the comfort zone, we can replace the word "information" with other motivators: 40–70% of experience, 40–70% reading or learning, 40–70% confidence, or 40–70% of planning. While we're completing the task, we'll also be doing analyzing and planning on the fly, so this range of certainty helps us tend toward action.

When you try to achieve more than 70% information (or confidence, experience, etc.), your lack of speed can result in many negative consequences. It can also destroy your momentum or stem your interest, effectively meaning nothing's going to happen. There is a high likelihood of gaining nothing further from surpassing this threshold.

For example, let's say you're opening up a cocktail bar, which involves buying a lot of different types of liquor. You can't expect to have absolutely all the liquor you will ever need ready when the doors are ready to open. But on the other hand, it doesn't make sense to commence operations without enough for customers to choose from.

So you'd wait until you have at least 40% of available inventory. You've got momentum established. You figure if you could get more than half of what you need, you'll be in pretty good shape to open. You might not be able to make absolutely every drink in the bartender's guide, but you'll have enough on-hand to cover the staple drinks with a couple of variations. If you have around 50–60% inventory, you're probably ready. When the remaining inventory arrives, you'll already be in action and can just incorporate that new inventory into your offerings. If you waited until you had 70% or more inventory, you could find yourself stuck in neutral for longer than you wanted to be.

This way of thinking leads to more action than not. Waiting until you have 40% of what you need to make a move isn't a sedentary stay inside your comfort zone—you're actively planning what you need to do to get out, which is just fine (as long as it's not over-planning). Making the execution before you're 100%—or even halfway—ready to do so is the kind of gutsy move that shakes you out of the indifference of your comfort zone in a hurry.

Have a Way to Undo Your Decision (If You Can)

The theme of this chapter has been to seek action slightly prematurely—even at the risk of overlooking a factor or two. Of course, our goals are to exit the comfort zone more consistently and reliably, so we must err on the side of action.

But every once in a while, you're going to jump into something that just doesn't work out. You might already be well into the task that you made the decision to do but might realize that it's not going to produce a satisfying result. This happens all the time at all levels of existence.

Part of the calculus of taking action is to take this into account and factor in exit strategies, costs, and the *undo-ability* of your decisions.

It's important to understand that admitting a wrong course of action is *not* failure, which is an emotion our comfort zones are expressly set up to deny. It was just something that didn't work out the way you intended. Coping with that errant path doesn't entail retreating into the confines of your comfort zone—it just means trying something new again.

If you've taken action but feel uneasy with it, start examining what the cost would be if you undid it. Try to have an exit strategy mapped out beforehand. Can you get home early from where you are planning to go if you want to (even if it costs extra)? Can you take a year's sabbatical in case you change your mind about leaving it? How much would it cost to move again if you hated where you live? Making a change could be painful and costly, but it helps to have everything arranged so you could do it if you have to.

Talk a few sentences about mapping out the costs for undoing something and how much it might set you back and how to be okay with that. Almost no decisions are permanent; some just have costs to undo, and some have virtually no costs at all to undo. Knowing this reality about how easy it is to undo relatively rash decisions is valuable, as it will allow you to make more "rash" decisions without worry of repercussions, and taking action is what this chapter is all about.

You might have to do some inventory at this point: budgeting the costs for canceling something and knowing how much it sets you back. That's something you have to be okay with. There's no such thing as a permanent, unchangeable decision (just as there's no such thing as perfection). There are only the efforts and relative costs of changing or stopping an act. Even with some "rash" decisions, you may not have that much to undo to get back to where you started. You may have so little to clean up, that you'll be less afraid to make those rash decisions in the future.

There's no shame—or at least there shouldn't be—about altering or canceling a course before you've finished it. It's not a sign of failure. Over the years, Google—one of the cornerstones of almost everyone's Internet experience that won't go away any time soon—has designed several new products and programs that don't exist anymore (anyone remember Google Wave? SideWiki? Jaiku?). Pulling the plug on those programs may have bummed out their developers, but it didn't mean their original impetuses were off-base or ill-founded. It just meant they didn't work in that particular framework. And none of their failures fatally stabbed Google in the heart.

There's a stigma about "jumping the gun" or doing things prematurely and not being fully ready to engage in a new course of action. We fear that without full and proper training, prep or awareness, our project will just collapse in a heap. But chances are remote of that fatality actually happening. What's more conceivable is that you'll feel more of a natural push or momentum to keep going when you *do* encounter occasional hiccups. You'll be learning on the job as all of us had to do at some point or another. Depending on your enterprise, you may want to consider jumping into the deep end of the pool, even if you haven't completely finished fastening your life jacket.

Takeaways:

1. Perfectionism isn't just procrastination; perfectionism is a story you tell yourself to ensure that you never get launched. But let's face the facts: your standards aren't the issue. It's your unwillingness to subject yourself to scrutiny from others.

2. Planning paralysis is when you become enamored with the preparation and planning as another form of procrastination that ultimately allows you to avoid action. It's sneaky!

3. The 40–70 rule states that you should have no fewer than 40% of the necessary information yet no more than 70% before

taking action or making a hard decision. This errs on the side of action but also ensures that you aren't just shooting from the hip.

4. Action is preferred, but action is scary. Therefore, part of the assurance you can make to yourself in taking action is to actively think about the costs for backing out and reversing decisions.

Chapter 5. Stay on Your Toes

The inconvenient truth of breaking out of your comfort zone is that it's inherently uncomfortable. But just like we can adapt to harsher weather or wet socks on a rainy day, being better with discomfort is a matter of practice.

This process seeks to turn a stabbing pain into a dull annoyance you can barely feel or a hunger pang that you actually crave because it means you are sticking to your diet. Making a regular habit of embracing uncomfortable situations can have a positive impact on all aspects of your life.

This chapter focuses on strategies to become better with discomfort, unpredictability, and generally losing control over your life. You'll learn that things will be okay after all, and that you don't have to fear something just because it is unknown. If you're numb to the temperature of the pool water, you'll slowly be able to go straight to the deep end on a consistent basis.

Stoicism

The Stoics espouse an idea that sounds contradictory but is valuable: practice voluntary discomfort. They practiced the act of deliberately getting uncomfortable to be better off in the future. This is the equivalent of intentionally going to the gym and hitting only your weakest muscles for days in a row.

What the Stoics sought was tranquility of mind. They wanted to stay calm in the face of adversity. True to their very name, they wanted to exude a basis of inner peace, no matter what trials or hardships manifested in their lives.

To do that, they advocated preparing for tough situations in advance—while everything in their lives was, relatively speaking, easy. They advised their acolytes to toughen up before the shit hit the fan, so to speak. They thoroughly trained themselves to become people who could do what everyone else dreaded doing. Additionally, they tried to *resist* doing what everyone else couldn't.

The reasoning behind it should make at least some sense: what we fear about hard situations is their uncertainty. So exposing yourself to the tough elements will result in your knowing what you're in for. It might even turn out to be less terrible than you thought it'd be. You realize things are not as bad as you have built them up to be, and discomfort is usually fleeting and an unworthy obstacle.

Putting yourself through certain trials while you still have control over them—when you're a *semi*-comfort zone—can help you withstand the elements that await you once you're completely outside it. When you encounter a situation that looks uncomfortable, you'll have that much more mettle to make it at least a little easier to endure.

Seneca, one of the most important Stoic philosophers (along with Marcus Aurelius and Epictetus), offered a sort of program for practicing the rigors of stoicism. It doesn't quite reduce itself to almost barren asceticism, but it does strip back the cozy comforts we've grown accustomed to:

> Set aside a certain number of days, during which you shall be content with the scantiest and cheapest fare, with coarse and rough dress, saying to yourself the while: "Is this the condition that I feared?" It is precisely in times of immunity from care that the soul should toughen itself beforehand for occasions of greater stress, and it is while Fortune is kind that it should fortify itself against her violence. In days of peace the soldier performs maneuvers, throws up earthworks with no enemy in sight, and wearies himself by gratuitous toil, in order that he may

be equal to unavoidable toil. If you would not have a man flinch when the crisis comes, train him before it comes.

The aim of Seneca's teaching is to make the student immune to discomfort. No matter what gets thrown his way, the student doesn't flinch, because he's already endured it and knows a large part of what to expect. You train yourself to be courageous in the process. After all, you had the courage to endure something uncomfortable willingly, so now you'll be able to recall that courage for difficult situations in the future. Fear is, after all, rooted to the unknown. If you present and expose yourself to that unknown, then you'll see how little there is to actually fear.

Stoic follower Cato the Younger—a senator in the late Roman Republic renowned for his utter incorruptibility and ethical code— practiced voluntary discomfort like nobody else. His almost obsessive composure was apparent from an early age. Cato simply refused to betray any hint of being ruffled or discomposed, even under threat of physical harm from older men who couldn't deal with his self-control.

As a young man Cato was rarely seen around Rome without his brother, Caepio, as company. Caepio was well regarded around town for his forbearance and moderation—but compared to Cato, he was practically lavish. Cato refused almost all comforts, no matter how trivial. When Caepio availed himself of ointments and perfumes, Cato flatly declined them. "When I compare myself with Cato," Caepio famously said, "I find myself scarcely different from Sippius," referring to townsman known for luxurious indulgence.

Cato wore unusual clothing for the sole purpose of experiencing people laughing at him. He walked barefoot and bareheaded in all weather. He traveled by foot alongside the horses that others rode. He ate the diet of a poor man, even as he himself had wealth, and often took long leave of retirement from the outside world, especially when sick.

This man didn't just accept abject circumstances—he *pursued* them, endured them, and let them inform his philosophical view. Cato also developed a tough resolve. When he got into an altercation at a public bath when another man struck him, he refused the man's apology after the fight was broken up. "I don't even remember being hit," he claimed.

Cato embraced the Stoic philosophy with nearly every fiber. His wealth, station, and reputation afforded him many comforts that he steadfastly refused. Cato practiced that austerity in almost every component of his life.

There's not much occasion, nor even practicality, to exercise this kind of stringent, almost bare-bones existence on an ongoing basis. But if anything is outside the comfort zone, it's Cato's program—imagine how little Cato would have to fear and how much it would take for him to refuse an action. He made himself bulletproof, and there are at least some ideas that we can draw from his way of life that we can put into practice.

Understand what you're doing when living within reduced means: you're not practicing self-denial, and you're not impoverished. You're just trying a way of life that encourages you to be more resourceful in your decisions and actions. You're practicing self-control in matters where all the answers are considered easily obtainable. Build your tolerance to discomfort on a small, daily level, and it will make you far more resilient to breaking out of your daily comfort zone. It may seem like Cato went to great lengths to punish himself, but he truly was only making himself stronger.

It's easy enough to deprive yourself of certain rich or expensive foods. But what about other comforts we take for granted that not all people enjoy? This could be as simple as taking public transit to work or even walking. It can be refusing to spend money on big-ticket items altogether for a while or using various versions of the concept of Lent and depriving yourself of a vice like chocolate or alcohol.

Here are some other ways we can practice Cato's model of deprivation in the present day:

- Give up TV for a month. Your favorite shows probably aren't going anywhere.

- Make a budget showing how much money you'll need for food over a given period of time—then slash it by 25% or even more, if you can.

- Unplug from social media for an extended time.

- Walk everywhere, in good weather or bad.

- Like Cato, don't invest in anything more than what you need for basic hygiene and presentability.

- Cut out every single form of advertising in your personal space for a while—junk mail, commercial television, or even most websites.

These sacrifices might sound exceptionally rough in these days of convenience and accessibility.

What's the point of this, again? Remember what the proposition of stoicism entails: living as if you were poor, intentionally depriving yourself of pleasure, and giving up comfort—so nothing is outside your comfort zone.

Resist Your Urges

It's interesting to consider how Cato would have preserved his ethics in contemporary Western society, where it's extremely easy for anyone to satisfy their urges. Indeed, we would find it almost *odd* if we weren't able to find instant solutions for our every desire. As punk artist Jello Biafra once ironically fantasized, "The happiness you have demanded is now *mandatory*."

Cato pursued a life of eliminating urges, but in our time there's almost no escape from our internal impulses or the actions and matters that can satisfy them immediately. But learning to exhibit self-control in acquiescing to sudden cravings is an obvious way to chip away at your comfort zone.

Zen priest Susan O'Connell has a favorite meditation instruction that you can adapt to any activity you can think of:

> When you're meditating and you feel like getting up, don't; then when you feel the urge to get up a second time, don't; and when you feel the urge to get up a third time, then get up. So you sit through the urge, the discomfort, twice before finally giving in the third time. This is a nice balance so that you're pushing your comfort zone a little.

Applying this technique to any kind of impulse should be easy enough to execute. If you sense a sudden desire for a nighttime snack, acknowledge the urge—but do nothing. When it happens a second time, do the same. Finally, after you've experienced, acknowledged, and maybe even reflected on the urge for a third time, go ahead and grab yourself some food. Feel your urges, and push them back at least twice before giving in.

As O'Connell says, this forces you to undergo the physical and mental sensation of the urge, pushing your endurance just enough to bring you in contact with the irritation of *not* gratifying yourself. A minor detail, to be sure—but if it's something you practice over and over for a longer time period, the overall effects could be cumulative and profound.

You can try this technique with anything. If you're exercising and looking forward to stopping on your 20th rep, take it to 30. Then push it to 40. Then stop—if you really want to. You can use this same method to temporarily hold off any other urges you might experience during a regular day: shopping, drinking, even talking.

By forcing yourself to endure a flash moment of discomfort, you start to understand the cunning nature of urges as they happen. Over time, you may not even feel the physical itch of the urge at all. You may become so immune to the discomfort that you might have to adjust the boundaries of your comfort zone! You'll be readier to try harder on a consistent basis.

Flexibility and Spontaneity

In our comfort zone, everything goes according to plan. Plans make us secure. Knowing what we're in for in a certain situation is always a source of reassurance. And there's no reason you shouldn't at least consider your ideas of how a certain activity or circumstance will play out.

But what happens when your plans fly out the window? Some outside force or disturbance renders your careful preparations totally useless, and your rigid designs aren't going to help you now.

In this instance, you have no choice but to be flexible and react to the spontaneity of the moment. If your Plan A has fallen by the wayside, you're going to have to consider your rarely used Plan B, C, or even the much-dreaded Plan D. These plans are going to lead you even further out of the comfort zone than you had originally intended.

Holding firmly onto prescribed plans isn't always the best idea to begin with. Being rigid too often can blind you to opportunities that might crop up out of nowhere. It also keeps you from living in the moment because you're commiserating about how your plans have collapsed.

But comfort with flexibility over well-laid plans can prepare you for any sudden movements and surprises. It forces you away from your routines and habits and helps you embrace the new ideas and experiences you can only find outside the comfort zone. Becoming comfortable with spontaneity is another muscle to be exercised.

Being flexible gives you a lot more options. Flexibility means seeing through different perspectives, tolerating ambiguity, taking chances, and learning from mistakes. Our environment is constantly changing, and maintaining a flexible attitude shows how we can handle diversity and other people's preferences. That, in turn, leads to openness, more opportunities, and more connections— not to mention decreases in depression and anxiety.

Think of flexibility as, in a way, the opposite of the resistance to urge we just discussed. It's seeing and following the path of least resistance—or, as your parents' bohemian friend would call it, "going with the flow." Following the currents that are part of the natural rhythm of a given situation is the easiest way to adapt to it.

Being inflexible actually creates a field of resistance that winds through every turn. Refusing to compromise to the will of the moment, or others around you, immediately cuts off your access from other ideas. You'll have a hard time existing, let alone thriving. In business situations, you might be perceived as a firm leader—but not a very productive one. You'll have a hard time getting others to share your vision.

When you allow yourself to be flexible, you'll better see where the river is leading. You can assume the shape that will carry you downstream. Maybe you won't agree with every single current or detail along the way—but you'll get downstream. You'll go somewhere. You just have to jump in the river.

A big part of flexibility is clearing out your preconceptions and expectations. The great martial artist Bruce Lee suggested, "Empty your mind. Be formless, shapeless—like water. Now you put water into a cup, it becomes the cup. You put water into a bottle, it becomes the bottle. You put it in a teapot, it becomes the teapot. Now water can flow or it can crash. Be water, my friend."

There are several ways we can incorporate a new attitude of flexibility in our everyday relationships and situations:

Eliminate "wrong" beliefs. One cause of inflexibility can be the beliefs that have been instilled in our lives—specifically, those that told us certain things were "wrong" and had to be avoided. "That group of people is trouble, so stay away from them." "That way of thinking is incorrect—don't pay any attention to it."

If you want to break out of the comfort zone, that's not the kind of approach to take. You have to think about how the widest cross section of people will appreciate your ideas and how you might need to adjust some of them to be effective. You have to consider all points of view to know what others' concerns or predilections are. Shutting out certain elements because of outdated, over-traditional, or just inaccurate dogma isn't the way to chart your life.

Openly court what you've believed to be "wrong." We're not talking about crimes, abuse, or illegality, of course. We mean viewpoints, traditions, or issues that you've had resistance to or have never really given serious consideration. Engage people and opinions outside of your own immediate worldview, whether informed by religious, political, social, or other "prisms." Learn about everyone and everything that's in your landscape. They're closer than they might appear.

Don't say "no" purely out of habit. Some people are inclined, maybe even proud, of their propensity to say "no." Rejection is a powerful destructor, and sometimes it's the easiest way to display a powerful appearance. But saying "no" out of habit isn't a very strong tactic for growth or experience.

Instead of thinking of 20 reasons not to do something new, think of five reasons why you *should*. There's plenty of things that will keep you from exercising, reading difficult material, trying a new cuisine, or any activity that involves a new kind of thinking or motion on your part. A lot of them will sound the same across the board—"too busy," "too much work," "too far to travel." Those excuses show up in practically all examples. But thinking of just five good reasons to say yes to something will usually result in responses unique to every different activity—and will heighten your anticipation for them.

Before issuing a routine denial, try to find the bigger picture and bring it to mind. Our no's are frequently issued quickly, dismissively, and without too much in the way of serious consideration. Rather than deny something outright, think of the larger context of the thing you're about to say no to.

For example, I might not feel like going out with friends, but I want to continue to build friendships and networks. I might not be excited about going to an art exhibit, but I want to deepen my appreciation for art. I might not want to sit through to my children's music recital at school, but I want to support my kids in their creative activities.

Saying yes to something you might have previously said no to in a knee-jerk way is a great means to expand your interests and travel outside your comfort zone. It usually feels better to say yes anyway.

Do your normal activities—with modifications. Normally, I do my writing while sitting on my couch (or reclining on it, like I am now). It works. It's relatively productive. But every once in a while, I'll take my laptop and go to a local coffee shop and bat out a few pages there. The view is different. Sometimes I get new ideas through just the smallest amount of people-watching.

It's not just a nice break from routine to do so; it's also flexibility training. Some of us do so much of a certain activity in exactly the same way in exactly the same place that we lead ourselves to believe that we can only do it in exactly that situation and setting. But that's not always true, and it can lead you to associate your work or routine with rut and over-familiarity. It's not hard to see how that reduces the potency and effectiveness of what you do.

Bringing what you normally do into a new situation immediately shifts some of your most dyed-in-the-wool perceptions of your routine. If you take the same route for your morning jog every day, try it tomorrow with a detour down a path or street you don't normally travel. (Then find your way back!) If you work in an office with open cubicle seating, sit in a different spot each day of one week. Listen to something other than your go-to radio station on your drive home. Take your kids to a park across town that they've never been to.

Even the slightest variance to your ordinary life can reveal new things, and you are simultaneously leaving your comfort zone in small, safe ways.

Utilize randomness. Remember Cato the Younger? We're not exactly sure how this truly transpired, but from time to time when he lost a bet, the winner got to choose what Cato was about to eat for dinner. Even when the winner conceded and told Cato to eat whatever he wanted, he insisted on not choosing himself. "Venus's decision," he'd say—whatever that means.

On a bigger, potentially less appetizing level, Cato deliberately sacrificed control over a certain decision and left it to the caprices of someone else. Whatever random choice his opponents made, by God, that's what he was going to have.

Randomness is not often described as a quality or positive trait for anything. Most of us try to avoid it in practical situations. But it's far more useful than one might think.

When I find myself in a situation where I can't make up my mind, I made the decision at random. For instance, I used to have a hard time deciding which of three or four movies I wanted to go see on a certain night. Now I just use an online random number generator and get a satisfactory direction in seconds.

Randomness is a great way to get yourself into the habit of arriving at a decision more quickly, saving you from the trouble of overanalyzing a bunch of factors—many of which don't end up meaning much at all in the final analysis. Random number generators, flipping a coin, tossing dice, or picking names out of a hat works for an unexpectedly wide range of decisions. When you can't decide what kind of soup to buy, what song to do at karaoke, or even what color to dye your hair, leaving at least that one small decision to fate is a great way to eliminate mitigating elements.

The principles and approaches in this chapter might be the most direct strikes you can make against the walls of your comfort zone. What better way to combat the placidity of comfort than to seek out *dis*comfort? It's a daring statement of nerve, proof of your dedication to changing the inactivity you cultivate in your safe surroundings. Once you're outside the comfort zone, you'll already have much of the stamina you'll need to endure.

Takeaways:

1. Breaking out of your comfort zone is an exercise in discomfort and pain. Therefore, we should exercise the mental muscles involved in dealing with such feelings.

2. Stoicism represents the first method to deal with discomfort because they encouraged practicing voluntary discomfort. They believed that fear was rooted in a lack of experience; therefore, exposure to all manners of discomfort would make one more resilient and immune to negative emotions. This makes your comfort zone grow exponentially.

3. Similarly, feeling and resisting urges at least twice before giving in is a practice in discipline and discomfort.

4. Finally, becoming comfortable with flexibility and spontaneity is important because of the lack of control. If you can

become accustomed to the feeling of controlled chaos by utilizing techniques such as randomness, eliminating "wrong" beliefs, and not saying no out of habit, you'll become far more likely to say "so what?" and break out of your comfort zone.

Chapter 6. Create an Alter Ego

Have you ever put on a mask for Halloween? Everyone you came in contact with that day knew you were wearing a mask. They might have even known it was you behind it. But admit it: wasn't it just the least bit *empowering*?

You might have felt, however rightly or not, that you couldn't be held responsible for what you did or said, because you could just blame it on the role later. "That wasn't me! That was Captain Jack Sparrow!" "I didn't eat all the snacks—that was Fat Albert! He eats everything!"

Of course, those excuses don't hold up after the fact. But when you're playing a role, especially if you have the costume to go with it, you probably take on a little bit of your character's traits and mannerisms. And it probably comes very easily.

One of the best ways to exit the comfort zone is by creating an alter ego because of the surprising feeling of power and control it can give you. During Halloween, you might feel emboldened and empowered—imagine how great it would be to apply that sort of feeling to everyday situations.

The Power of (Perceived) Anonymity

Anonymity gives us a sense of bravery, and this is best showcased in today's social media and online world. When we lurk behind a fictitious screen name, we unchain ourselves from the restrictions of our own, real-world identities. We speak through another voice, almost like a ventriloquist speaks through the dummy on his lap. We may express things we'd never say in the real world. This is what scientists call the "online disinhibition effect."

(Of course, this is unfortunately why cyberbullying is so widespread as well. I should make it clear that nothing in this chapter should be taken as encouragement to bully anybody, online or otherwise.)

A recent survey conducted by the audience engagement platform Livefyre reinforces that conclusion. The company, which powers user-content features for major web entities, asked 1300 web users if they've ever commented anonymously online and why.

Most said they did so because they didn't want their opinions to impact their work or professional life by being attached to their real names. They also responded that they wanted what they *said*, the actual content of their message, to be the focus of the post rather than their identity. Almost 80% said if a site forced them to log in with their true identities, they wouldn't comment at all. Seems that perceived anonymity isn't just empowering; it's necessary for most people.

Arthur Santana, communications professor at the University of Houston, analyzed 900 randomly selected user comments on articles about immigration. Half of them were from newspapers that allowed anonymous posts, like the *Los Angeles Times* and the *Houston Chronicle*. The other half were from sources that did not allow anonymous posts, including *USA Today* and the *Wall Street Journal*. Santana found that anonymity had a huge effect on the comments' nature: 53% of the anonymous posters were "uncivil," whereas only 29% of registered, truly identified posters acted that way. The link between online namelessness and rudeness, Santana concluded, is unquestionable.

This is the same effect you can create (in a nicer way) when you create an alter ego. Alter egos can be a hidden side of your personality, an exaggeration of what you really believe, or someone totally opposite from who you are. The underlying point is that you feel exponentially more freedom, sensing yourself to be immune from retribution or harm in the real world.

For example, in real life you might be a blue-collar man who's an auto mechanic. Let's say you're a little tough on the outside, surely masculine, maybe a little macho. But boy oh boy, do you love *The Little Mermaid.* You saw the movie as a kid and it swept you away. You love the music, you love the comic characters, and you identify so completely with Arial that thinking about her almost makes you tear up inside.

Your daily auto-mechanic self might not necessarily show that side to your fellow workers. You might not feel like expressing your total adoration for *The Little Mermaid* on lunch break. But you can go online with the screen name WholeNewWorld182 and express your feelings to your heart's content, knowing you're among "friends" who'll understand the depth of your devotion.

This isn't the same thing as lying. You're telling the truth, just using a shielded identity to do so. And your hyper-manly fellow workers won't know about it. (They're probably *Beauty and the Beast* fans anyway.)

Used properly, an alter ego can help nudge you closer and closer to the edges of your comfort zone. It might be the most fun you can have doing so.

What Is an Alter Ego?

For our purposes, an alter ego is a second self created by an individual, usually for the purposes to live out a "better" version of the self.

In comic books, Bruce Wayne runs his multimillion-dollar business every day. Peter Parker works as a photographer for the *Daily Bugle*. But when a crisis hits the cities they live in and the usual authority figures are unable to handle it, they morph into their crime-fighting alter egos Batman and Spiderman. The city is saved, usually with a little property damage, but still saved.

Pop music artists, in particular, are frequent adopters of the alter ego. When they take the stage, they have to push out a larger-than-life spectacle that takes more than their everyday, regular selves to pull off. All pop musicians do that to some extent, but some go even further by creating elaborate personas.

For a time, the great British performer David Bowie changed personas seemingly at will. The best-known was Ziggy Stardust, a humanoid alien who's something of an extraterrestrial messenger. Ziggy let Bowie distance himself from the boy from Beckenham and take on a fearless, heroic personality.

In 2008 American singer and songwriter Beyoncé Knowles created her own alter ego, Sasha Fierce. This character was fun, sensual, glamorous, and aggressive—all of which were on full display in her video "Single Ladies." Apart from her Sasha persona, Beyoncé was reserved, polite, and genial. But her alter ego was the vehicle for singing and saying things that might not have been as effectively conveyed using her everyday image.

An alter ego encompasses the best parts of what you want to be and gives you full license to do what you couldn't do as yourself. At the very least, it allows you to ask what someone else would do and witness the separation between your answer to the same question.

Why an Alter Ego

You probably aren't a private citizen who turns into a valiant superhero or a pop superstar. So how can an alter ego serve to help you step out of your comfort zone?

When you're using an alias and acting outside your own character, you might find it easier to take action. You could lose all consciousness of yourself, including your fears and apprehensions. It's almost like training wheels for riding outside the comfort zone.

An alter ego that's thought out well can help you bridge the gap between where you are now and where you want to be. It lets you step out of the box you've created for yourself in public and do something that's totally out of character. The imaginative process you take in creating and being that alter ego might provide clues on how to make those improvements in your real life. Finally, it just lets you ask, "What would my fearless alter ego do?" which is a more productive question to answer than "What should I do here if I know I should be brave but am still scared?"

Having an alter ego, as we've mentioned, is empowering. After switching characters, you have a window of opportunity when you can be brave and detach yourself from your hang-ups. That window of time is when you push against your comfort zone and try new things.

Like Bowie did with Ziggy, you can channel your fearlessness through your alter ego. Sure, Bowie could have sung all the Ziggy songs dressed in a T-shirt and jeans while not wearing any makeup. But by taking on another character, Bowie turned those songs into a whole new drama with graspable themes, storylines, and excitement. It was a gambit that let him display his creativity to its fullest.

On a more serious note, an alter ego can give you some distance from yourself and help you deal better with the past, present, and future. When you think of your alter ego, you're more likely to make good decisions on their behalf. The self-distance and objectivity you create when taking on this alter ego, and thinking about what he or she would do, can sharpen your focus on the bigger picture and make some of your long-term goals a little clearer.

When it comes to the future, you might be more willing and eager to take on challenges if you picture your alter ego doing them instead of yourself. For the moment, your alt-self will be the one taking the chances, facing obstacles, and risking failure. It won't be you, for now. But when it finally becomes your turn, you'll be more prepared to handle it, thanks to what your alter ego set up for you.

The Alter Ego as Buffer for Your Real Ego

Every time you're about to try a new endeavor, there's a little voice in your head that begins whining and advising you. This is your actual ego, the one Freud described. Its job, as we discussed earlier, is to be the reasonable one in any new situation.

And when faced with a new situation, your ego gets a little jittery: "What are you doing??

Stop! What if you look stupid? What will everyone think? What if they all laugh at you? Who do you think you are, anyway—you're not brave or smart or strong enough to do this! Let's just go home and watch *The Little Mermaid* again!"

That's when an alter ego comes to the rescue, bolts past your ego's whimpering, and leads you out of the comfort zone. Where the ego expresses fear, the alter-ego is rarin' to go. "Hey! This looks great! This looks exciting! Let's get started now!"

The ego then says, "But what will everybody say? You're just setting this person up for ridicule!" To which the alter ego responds, "Oh, forget them. If they don't have anything better to do than gossip, let 'em talk. They can think whatever they want. It's not going to get in our way. I got no use for 'em."

Finally, the ego cries, "But what if I *fail*?" And the alter ego says, "If you try it, yeah, you might fail—but you might *succeed*. Whereas if you *don't* try, then you'll *definitely* fail. Excuse me, I'm running late."

Let's say you're starting a new job, for which you feel grateful but a little underqualified. Your ego is shaking in its boots—"I'm not ready for this! I can't do all the things they'll expect me to do!"

Your alter ego: "Fantastic! I can't wait to jump in! I'm going to take charge of this sucker—I'll be too busy to be bored!"

Ego: "But they'll be disappointed! They were expecting someone else with more experience and knowledge than I have!"

Alter Ego: "You bet they are—they're expecting *me*! And boy oh boy, are they gonna get me!"

Ego: "If I don't work out, they're going to fire me and I'm going to be destitute and broke! I can't do this!"

Alter Ego: "Oh, no they won't. I'm far too powerful for them. I can do anything. I can do several things at once. I can do *their* jobs as well! In fact, just for fun, I think I'm going to do just that! This is a funhouse of opportunity, and I'm knockin' on that door, baby!"

Your results—and inner dialogue—may vary. Not only are you speaking in the terms of your alter ego, but you're also treating your *comfort zone's* ego as an objective, other character as well. You can verbalize what it is about that comfort zone that you want to change and let your alter ego run with it.

How to Create Your Alter Ego

So you've decided you're going to don the cap or put on the breastplate—metaphorically speaking, probably—and indulge yourself in the character of an alter ego. How do you go about it?

Determine why you want an alter ego. Ask yourself what's spurring you to develop an alter ego and what you hope to achieve. Do you want to be more outgoing, confident, or unique? Do you need someone to stand up for you? Do you just want more people to read your blog or watch your YouTube videos? In what way will they be assisting in breaking you out of your comfort zone?

147

Your alter ego should have some sort of purpose or mission. Remember, you're looking for empowerment, an avenue by which you can express yourself in a new context. You're putting your hopes, dreams, fears, and insecurities into this alter ego, giving them the kind of abilities that you don't have as a mortal human. Your alter ego doesn't necessarily have to live by the rules, but it should have a *point*.

Develop your alter ego's personality. What type of person does your alter ego have to be to achieve the goals you're after? How do they think? What's their mindset? What models are you using to build their thoughts or actions?

You have an unlimited range of options to choose from. You could just use the alter ego as a reflection or extrapolation of yourself to imbue a personality that you'd like to someday inhabit. Conversely, you can make it your polar opposite to investigate a total contrast of yourself to help you understand the "other side." The answers you're looking for are largely going to come from the type of attitudes and voicing your alter ego has, so develop them as fully as you can.

Make sure you can describe your alter ego, without hesitation, using five positive adjectives. These are the traits you are striving toward.

Flesh out the details. The secondary part of your alter ego's story will be how they'd present themselves to the rest of the world— so give them a name and an appearance. Again, you have no restrictions here. You might be a T-shirt and jeans person, but your alter ego could be a high-fashion hound all the way with garish fur coats and sparkling sunglasses. Or perhaps they'll only wear black and disappear underneath the hood of their sweatshirt.

Spend time developing your alter ego's mannerisms. How do they walk? What does their voice sound like? How do they wear their hair, or do they wear hats? Do they speak the King's English or do they have some kind of accent? The more details you can provide for your alter ego, the easier it will be to slip into their character.

Try to come up with a significant and meaningful name. You can base it on someone you admire, the name of your superhero, a take on another fictional character, or one from history. You could just attach a superlative to the end of your name—"Felix the Great"—or spell your name backward. Have some sort of justification or explanation for the name, even if it's random. As with appearances, the more detail you can invent, the more tangible the alter ego will feel.

Activate! An alter ego should respond to some kind of call to action, something to invoke them when they're needed. Captain Marvel called out to his gods, who then graciously struck him with lightning and turned him into a superhero. Batman was channeled into action by an extremely powerful, custom-made flashlight that seemingly every household in Gotham had. The alter-ego rock band KISS took to the stage with the announcer's cry "You wanted the best . . . you *got* the best! The hottest band in the world, KISS!"

You could come up with a rallying cry, something that could theoretically fit on a T-shirt or hat. You could cue up a song that would announce the alter ego's arrival or something that would just pump you up. You could throw red roses in its pathway, unfurl a flag or carpet, clang on a cowbell—whatever works.

The activation routine is important because it's meant to snap you out of your mood and take on the alter ego's spirit. If you feel sad, it's extraordinarily difficult to just "decide" you feel happy. Some sort of catalyst, calling or benediction can help turn that alternate mood on.

Remember, this isn't just escapism. A lot of people do role-playing or cosplay for recreational reasons. While you should have fun with your alter ego, you're not just creating it to escape into a fantasy world. You invented it to figure out a solution of some sort to achieve a certain goal.

Ask yourself how your alter ego would act in the process of accomplishing your purpose. Give this a lot of very conscious thought. Then act that way. Create a distance from your own self and "storyboard" how your creation would perform in the situation at hand. How would James Bond deal with your overbearing boss? How would Gollum from *Lord of the Rings* make a marriage proposal? How would Darth Vader handle himself at your in-laws' Thanksgiving dinner?

You know how *you'll* act. That's why creating a distance from that is important. Your alter ego encourages you to act more quickly, more sharply, and more bravely because you're taking yourself out of the picture. You're not thinking about yourself anymore. You're thinking about a woodland nymph, an astronaut, Marilyn Monroe, and the Incredible Hulk now.

Takeaways:

1. The power of an alter ego has been shown in studies on online anonymity. If you can be vile and rude online as someone else,

imagine the positive potential of anonymity.

2. Your alter ego, to be most effective, should represent your ideal self, at least in the aspect of breaking out of your comfort zone. What do you wish you were more or less of? What traits are you seeking? That's what your alter ego should epitomize because you already know what *you'll* do in certain situations and it's something you want to change.

3. The alter ego serves as a buffer and counter to the ego—Freud's concept of what keeps us insulated from judgment and rejection.

4. The best alter egos are highly defined and detailed and also have an activation element—there must be a signal to snap you into your alter ego, so to speak. This is important because otherwise there is no way to easily disassociate from your everyday persona.

Chapter 7. Mission: Impossible

Here's a fact that I hope won't break your heart or shatter your illusions: everyone is normal.

The celebrities you see on stage and screen? Normal. The billionaires you read about in financial magazines and newspapers? Normal. Those athletes scoring multimillion-dollar contracts and product endorsements? Hopelessly normal.

You are *also* normal. There aren't any specially endowed people who make profits or championships appear from thin air. There are only people who work their tails off, repeatedly find and capitalize on opportunities, and maybe score a little bit of luck (through hustle and timing—nobody "just" gets lucky; they lay the groundwork for luck).

Don't tell yourself that people are born special. Ben and Jerry were a couple of directionless Vermonters who took a $5 correspondence course on the art of making ice cream. They opened an ice cream shop in a rundown, abandoned gas station. They slowly built a following and eventually got their product in local grocery stores. They worked to improve their craft and their sales acumen. Forty years later, their brand of ice cream is arguably the most well known in America.

Once again, Ben and Jerry learned this from a correspondence *course*. Not only were they not particularly special, but Ben didn't even have a sense of taste or smell—and became an ice cream magnate.

What's the point here? Everything is possible until proven impossible, especially in regard to what lies outside your comfort zone. Normal people do the impossible and frightening every day, so what are you waiting for?

This tenet might be so far away from your comfort zone it's practically in another zip code: occasionally we really need to exert and push ourselves to find out what we're capable of doing, and we can only truly do that if we aim for what appears to be fantastical or impossible.

If something looks impossible to you, that's a great sign that you should immediately start thinking how to make it possible. It's also great to get into the mindset of trying to understand why you're intimidated by it. You might discover that it strikes a chord with your feelings of inadequacy or insecurity.

Take this thing I'm doing right now—writing. When someone introduces themselves as a "writer," those who think that's an impressive title open their eyes wide. The word "writer" still has a mystical quality to it. It conjures up images of great novelists who were able to summon pearly words from the air down into their fingers like Dickens or Hemingway.

In fact, that's what I used to think about writers—and it was why I struggled with the notion that I couldn't do it. As a younger person, I thought writers were born with their talents and insights. They were things that just came naturally to them. So I was frustrated with the fact that I had to work on it. Surely my favorite authors didn't do that; for them, turning out page after page of genius was like turning on a tap for them.

But I learned that most of *them* felt the same way I did—once. And they worked themselves out of that thinking by researching, writing, rewriting, editing, re-editing, re-re-editing, and getting rejection letters for all their efforts. They weren't born writers after all. They were simply hard workers, and they paid attention to what they needed to do to improve.

A couple of friends of mine always said they were average-to-below-average writers. Writing intimidated them for some reason, so they went in different directions until each of them decided to start their own blogs—one about mental and physical health and the other about motherhood.

When their blogs went up, I visited each of them and couldn't believe how articulate, intelligent, and well constructed their writing was. Not because I didn't think they could do it, but because they'd told *me* several times that they couldn't do it. They started from a can't-do-it position, got tired of being there, then worked on their skill when nobody was watching. And now, they do it.

Whenever someone says that can't do something, they're reacting to insecurities or perceived inadequacies. But all that's standing between them and accomplishments is a trail of work. Because nobody's special— some just work. All that work reminds you how hard you believe in yourself and your ideas and reinforces that belief. Before you know it, after you've put in the time, you sit

159

back and realize you've accomplished the impossible.

The "Things I Can't Do" List

Start with completing a list of things you can't do, for whatever reason, no matter how big or small. Make sure it's not a "things I'm not very good at" list. What you're making, very specifically, is a list of things you *cannot* do under any circumstances.

Once you've finished your list, pick one item from it and go do it.

Okay, maybe it's not that simple. But you've at least attempted that just a few minutes ago you thought was impossible for you to do. Maybe you didn't a bang-up job—it might not have been an absolutely fantastic thing in the end. Maybe you only got halfway through. But you did it anyway. And now that you've done it once, you can go back and do it again. You got much closer than you thought you would, and it wasn't really a matter of not being able to do it, was it?

The more you realize you can do anything that you put your mind to, the more daring, bold, and audacious you'll be.

Let's go back to the list you made. Say your limitations out loud and then simply rebut them with an affirmation of what you *can* accomplish. Here's an example:

- I can't run a 5K race because I've never been athletic. *But I can finish it.*

- I can't draw because I'm not artistic. *But I can do it.*

- I can't take dance classes; I have two left feet. *But I can get through it.*

- I can't give a speech; I'm terrible at speaking in public. *But I won't die in a pool of sweat.*

Why make the "I can't" statements? Because it verbalizes what keeps you in your comfort zone. It helps you realize that you're being kept there because of your doubts—it's a negative. That right there should make you feel a little less comfortable.

Why follow it up with a "but" statement? Because it lessens the stress of having to accomplish too much. It gives you a floor of expectation that you know you won't disappoint. Just by removing that emotional blockage, you're making it easier to step outside the comfort zone (and maybe even surprise yourself.) It removes the all-or-nothing element you've used on yourself and makes the impossible actually possible.

Make the first step you have to take as easy as you can possibly make it. If you want to start going to the gym, the first step you can take is making a list of the gyms that are near your house or workplace.

This may seem like an insignificant step, but it's not. It's launching the idea in your head in a practical way, and it's important to acknowledge the barriers you've made for yourself. Whether you've been staying inside your comfort zone out of fear or perceived lack of ability, this challenges those notions.

But as mentioned before, we can't do this every day. We simply can't or we'll burn out quickly. You can't live outside of your comfort zone 24 hours a day. Every once in a while, you need to come back and process your experiences.

From time to time, you simply just need a break. Leaving the comfort zone is exciting, but it can also be exhausting and can have real adverse effects on your body and mind. Know when it's time to come home. When you feel a physical sense of exhaustion or fatigue setting in, mark your place and get back to where you can relax. The great thing about being outside the comfort zone is better appreciating what you have when you're *in* it.

Know Your Carrots and Sticks

Human beings are primarily motivated by the pursuit of pleasure and the avoidance of pain. This dichotomy of reward and punishment is represented by the metaphor of carrots and sticks. At our most basic level, we are just animals who learned how to walk upright and happened to develop opposable thumbs and larger brains. If we are able to pinpoint what truly motivates us in both negative and positive ways, achieving the impossible or scary becomes an afterthought.

The carrot—the reward—is offered or promised to those who act in the desired way. On the other hand, the stick is the punishment administered to those who *don't* act that way.

In terms of modern workplaces, "carrots and sticks" represents positive and negative motivation. Sticks—the negative—don't work as well. The motivation is short-lived; it's only in effect while the stick is there. Sticks don't do anything to reinforce our potential or encourage us to excel. They don't come from affirming or supportive stances either—after all, they're punishment.

Just as the stick is a construct for workplace fear that usually doesn't work, the presence of negative reinforcement doesn't help us move out of the comfort zone for too long. Our only motivation is to do just enough until the presence or threat of the stick goes away. Once we do it, our inclination is to head right back into comfort now that the immediate threat is over. It's not sustainable motivation to achieve the impossible.

However, too many carrots can also be a problem. They generate anticipation, excitement, and possibility. But an overdose of carrots invites laziness and lessens the incentive to work. This happens because frequently people get carrots for reasons other than merit or performance—they just get a regularly scheduled salary increase or get promoted just because of their seniority or other inconsequential factors.

With all these great carrots in our space, now we're *really* in our comfort zone. We're given so much for just being there and accomplishing the bare minimum. So in that situation, we think all we need to do is maintain status quo. Why try harder?

Too many sticks in a motivational system lead to retaliatory behavior from people. They result in grievances against management, the formation of labor unions, poor quality workmanship, incurably low morale, and other deleterious effects.

Everyone differs as to what works best. As you might expect, a wealth of studies has been conducted to investigate the relative merits and drawbacks of the carrot-and-stick methods and what will ultimately get you moving.

Hanneke den Ouden and Roshan Cools, with their colleagues from the Donders Institute in Nijmegen in the Netherlands and New York University, published their research in the journal *Neuron*. They concluded that a couple of brain chemicals, serotonin and dopamine, and related genes influence how we base our choices on past punishments and rewards.

Parts of the influence are based on the gene variants who inherited from your parents. "We used a simple computer game to test the genetic influence of the genes DAT1 and SERT, as these genes influence dopamine and serotonin," Den Ouden explained. "We discovered that the dopamine gene affects how we learn from the long-term consequences of our choices, while the serotonin gene affects our choices in the short term."

"Different players use different strategies. It all depends on their genetic material. People's tendency to change their choice immediately after receiving a punishment depends on which serotonin gene variant they inherited from their parents. The dopamine gene variant, on the other hand, exerts influence on whether people can stop themselves making the choice that was previously rewarded, but no longer is."

Even given the biological differences, the underlying point is that you need to find your motivators that will allow you to set impossible or frightening goals. How do we balance all the information about carrots and sticks?

You need to identify them, internalize them, and find a way to keep them uppermost in your mind. You must always have access to what is driving you onward. What is meaningful to you about what you want to achieve? What motivates you, makes you want to walk across burning coals to get it? What's in it for you—what's the carrot you're chasing and the stick you're escaping? Use both, and create them out of thin air if you must.

A possible "carrot" could be the promise of a raise or a bonus, some kind of promotion or advancement. If you prove yourself and work in the way superiors want you to, you'll be rewarded. A "stick," on the other hand, could be something as minor as the threat of demotion, a short-tempered manager, or even the loss of your job altogether. Other carrots include validation, feelings of security, approval, and love. Other sticks include fear, rejection, disappointment, and failure. Notice that the most effective ones are simple emotions.

Being totally clear on your carrots and sticks lets you be properly motivated and more likely to finish your job—even if it's outside your comfort zone. You're constantly reminding yourself what's at stake. Getting out of your comfort zone by itself might not be terribly strong motivation—you have to find the *reasons* you are doing something, root motives you won't admit to anybody else.

Knowing clearly what your sticks and carrots are—and which of them are real—increases your chances of accomplishing something impossible. You know what real rewards are possible by getting out of your comfort zone and what you truly face as a negative consequence.

For example, why are you the only person spending your night hours on a project for work? Maybe you're trying to prove yourself because you're terrified of being unemployed. Or maybe you feel like you've never been able to live up to your supervisor's lofty standards. Or maybe it's just that you don't want to go home.

It's probably obvious why taking on what we fear, or trying to achieve the impossible, chips away at the walls of your comfort zone. What's not always obvious are the forces that hold you back or the forces that make you too satisfied or content to take a chance. You have to dig down and bring those core beliefs into scrutiny and examine how each of them provoke your interest or stun your incentive. That awareness is another piece of equipment that makes bursting out of your comfort zone more meaningful.

Takeaways:

1. We're all normal, yet normal people appear to do the impossible or frightening every day. So what's it to you? Your turn is coming.

2. A large part of what holds us back are the limiting beliefs about our abilities. This can be easily shown when creating an "I can't do" list. Adding a "but" statement at the end is a powerful way to show that you can indeed do something, just not to the arbitrary standard you were holding yourself to. It is direct evidence that it is not impossible or even scary.

3. Carrots and sticks are important in the sense that they can decimate a comfort zone by themselves. Carrots are positive

reinforcers, while sticks are negative reinforcers—essentially rewards and punishments, respectively. If you can be clear enough about what motivates you from both aspects—negative and positive—you just might have enough to bypass your fears and doubts.

Chapter 8. Comfort Zone Busting Methodologies

We've dived deeply into the science, philosophies, and general strategies for breaking out of your comfort zone. This chapter will introduce you to three step-by-step methods that can help you really do something new.

Having a system or plan is always good for something that can seem a little abstract. Personal change is certainly one of those efforts that can seem daunting from a distance, especially when we're dealing with ways to change our thinking or approach to lives. Especially with a pursuit loaded with potential anxiety and boldness as leaving your comfort zone, steps that have been proven to work are always helpful. Simply put, blueprints are always helpful, especially with something you have fear and hesitation about.

These systems are great ways to frame your thoughts, emotions, and motivations for moving toward the edges of your comfort zone. They allow you to take fearful situations and approach them with a courageous mindset or to know what elements to look for when evaluating situations.

The Three C's

Andy Molinsky is the author of *Reach: A New Strategy to Help You Step outside Your Comfort Zone, Rise to the Challenge and Build Confidence.* He's also a professor of psychology and organizational behavior at Brandeis University's International Business School. He's a busy man.

Molinsky explained that he'd discovered three common elements used by people who step outside their comfort zones successfully. He refers to these mechanisms as the three C's: conviction, customization, and clarity.

Conviction. This is the deeply held belief that the action that's going to lead you out of the comfort zone is worth the hard work it entails. Conviction includes knowing your own motivations—why taking this action is important to you. It forms the basis of your motivation and reinforces your own personal justifications for pushing through efforts that might be uncomfortable, or at least inconvenient, to get to a higher goal.

Andy uses himself as an example. The promotional work an author has to do—making public appearances, giving interviews—is outside of Andy's comfort zone. He probably prefers the writing part of it much more. But promo tours are necessary functions in the process of publishing a book. It's worth it to him because of his end goals and motivations. Andy does appearances because he's convinced his book can help

175

people lead better lives, and they're how he raises awareness of his book directly to those people.

Customization. This is the art of tweaking or adjusting how you perform a task—even just slightly—to make it feel more comfortable and natural to your unique sensibilities. Customization need not be a major overhaul; in fact, it's better not to approach it that way. They're simply small modifications that make the task feel more like something you own. They're small but not insignificant reminders that you are the one steering the efforts and that you're bringing something of yourself to them. They're signatures you leave for yourself.

For example, if you want to push yourself to speak up at a meeting, you don't have to emulate Tony Robbins or some other speaker. What's your style, and how can you incorporate that into your speech? If you're a joker, make jokes. If you're serious, be serious. If you tend to be comfortable while drawing, draw the entire time. None of these actions may be perceptible to your peers, but they give you just enough of an edge to help you feel more powerful and confident.

One reason stepping out of the comfort zone is so fearful is because we feel helpless and have a sense of not being in control. By customizing portions of the event, you'll regain at least a fraction of that control that you'll find empowering.

Clarity. Sometimes in our travels outside the comfort zone, we might occasionally let some irrational thoughts sneak in and take over. These come in the form of negative ruminations: "This will be utter failure," "I'm going to fall face first on the pavement and everyone will see it happen," "If I can't do this perfectly, there's no point in my doing it." It's obvious how these kinds of thoughts can paralyze you before you even start.

When it happens, you need to tag them as the irrational thoughts they are—and then go after some clarity.

Clarity is developing an even-handed, level-headed perspective on the challenges you face. It's stopping yourself from giving into

177

the distorted, exaggerating thinking that stops us dead in our tracks in stressful moments.

Once those irrational thoughts show up, counter them with other statements: "Everything's going to be fine," "Even if things go wrong, it won't be the end of the world," "I don't have to be perfect—I just have to do the best I can."

How do you incorporate the three C's?

You want to start a soup kitchen in your community to feed your neighbors that have fallen on hard times. But first you have to appear in front of a charity commission to get permission to build it and hopefully get some financial assistance.

What's your conviction? You've lived in your community for years, have extremely close ties within it, and have seen it go through some difficult economic circumstances. You feel it's extremely vital to preserve the community.

How about customization? Well, nobody's seen you when you're not in casual clothes, so you'll have to dress up a little bit for the presentation. But you might wear a necktie (or scarf, or pin, or whatever) that's in the colors of the high school in the community. You can do this for luck, or to show personal expression, or to advertise the community you serve.

As for the clarity component, you realize that the committee may turn you down. But at the very least you'll bring awareness of the crisis to the board members and maybe even established relationships with them for a future opportunity. You counteracted your fears about what *might* happen with certainty about what *did* happen and what your reasons were. Those facets will never change—you're clear about them.

The three C's approach teaches the perspective of imparting meaning to your actions and letting that meaning carry you into scary waters.

The 2 AM Principle

Most of the issues we've covered in this book involve breaking out of the comfort zone to make personal accomplishments or solve problems. But doing so to have an amazing experience—dare we say it, actual *fun*—can tap into the same element of risk and daring as more serious exploits. This approach is more about how to actively seek territories outside of your comfort zone rather than expanding your current one.

Jon Levy is a behavioral scientist whose personal focus is to make lives more adventurous. His book, *The 2 AM Principle: Discover the Science of Adventure*, is a treatise on how to transform ordinary lives into rollicking series of escapades. "Nothing good happens after 2am," he says, "except the most EPIC experiences of your life."

Levy's traveled extensively in pursuit of adventure. He was trampled by a bull in Pamplona, Spain. He's played a spirited and intense game of Jenga with Kiefer Sutherland. He's crashed a bachelorette party by jumping into a limo full of strangers. He's got spunk, in other words.

Levy discovered three elements to something being a bona fide adventure:

- The experience was worth talking about. It could have been a visit to a spectacular-looking canyon or a barroom where everyone was on their wildest behavior.

- It carried a sense of adversity or perceived risk. This could be a physical risk like high-diving or a personal risk like shot-taking, pole-dancing, or karaoke-singing.

- It made you a different person after it was over. A skydive that turned you into someone afraid of nothing or a conversation with a stranger that changed your mind.

Although I've given you examples of activities that covered each of those elements, the trick is finding an activity that has *all three of them.*

Levy's not talking about leisure time or "fun." He's not talking about bowling or going roller-skating. (Though, he *could* be talking about bowling in the middle of a roller-skating rink.) For Levy, "fun" is always enjoyable, but it's shallow—it's something comfortable and unchallenging that you do to relax. That's comfort zone territory.

What Levy talks about are precarious situations that present an element of danger but push the safety or acceptability boundaries just enough so they'll ramp up the risk—but not break. It could be a drag race, crashing a fashion show, or traveling alone to a foreign country where you can't understand the language, know no one, and don't necessarily have strict plans about where you're going to crash.

One kind of adventure that could fit Levy's model could be something as genial as a dinner party. Levy told *Elle* magazine how he has a monthly dinner party with five friends, none of who know each other. Instead of going out to dinner, they hit the supermarket, picked up food, and cooked together in his kitchen—definitely an experience worth talking about, one that could court failure because of the uncertainty of the strangers and one that changed all the guests because they probably made four new friends in one shot.

Levy realizes that not everyone has time or means to pursue his more edgy activities—so to compensate, he gives four elements that can turn an ordinary event into an extraordinary one:

Team. Levy builds a social team the way managers assemble a work team—as evenly a gender ratio as he can get, with different backgrounds, communication styles, approaches, and experience. "A great group can make the most awful location fun."

Movement. Levy's adventures aren't stationary. They tend to be moveable feasts or fetes simply to change the scenery as often as possible. "Your brain operates differently when you change location."

Mission. There's always a point to the adventure, whether it's a physical goal or a more intangible, emotional one. From a distance, it may seem like a reckless mob, but if there's at least some goal to it, then a nice context forms. "This drives group behavior, causes outsiders to want to join, and helps you get out of your comfort zone."

Constraints. These are certain conditions or rules that participants in the adventure adhere to—anything from visiting only certain kinds of bars to playing games where you get strangers to buy you drinks. "We get the most enjoyment from activities just outside of our skill zone."

Levy gave the example of how he arranged a group of friends for a night of bar-hopping. The invitees were all from different backgrounds (team). They agreed to spend no more than one hour in any spot (movement). They wanted to make it the most monumental night out in the history of New York (mission). They also made vows *not* to go to any bar they were familiar with and to say yes to anything anybody offered, except drugs (constraints).

Adventure is a key, but often overlooked, component of life outside the comfort zone. Levy's 2 AM principle offers an interesting way to structure and view the wild side and amazingly make it mean more.

Higher Performance Through Adventure

Author Matt Walker provides another piece of mythology for quality comfort zone busting. His website boasts the headline "High Performance Living Happens Through Adventure." He ascribes several qualities to an adventure that reflect components of our daily lives and survival.

Adventure is high endeavor. It's the ability to think big and bigger about you who are, how you live, and what you can do in the world. These kinds of aspirations only come into view when we escape the comfort zone and see the opportunity that surrounds us.

Adventure is total commitment. How willing you are to embrace challenge as you move toward success—knowing that it doesn't mean you have to have blind faith or brash neglect but that it means having confidence and belief in the face of challenge. Commitment is the grounding element that pushes us through completing the adventure to its full extent.

Adventure has an uncertain outcome. Knowing how something's going to end makes it no more of an adventure than a roller coaster or a packaged tour group. Life is nothing if not uncertain—so you might as well get comfortable with it. There may be adversity and unease, but an uncertain outcome also offers the gift of possibility. Remember how acknowledgment of the unknown is a prime mover for getting out of the comfort zone.

Adventure is tolerance for adversity. It measures our resilience in unfamiliar or challenging situations—whether we can still use humor and exhibit grace in tough moments. We also get the opportunity to step back and accept the sometimes absurd aspects of being human, admiring and embracing it for what it is, and moving on. When we can encounter elements, people, or conditions that contrast with our own and appreciate the differences, we've gained levels of understanding we can't get within the comfort zone.

Adventure is great companionship. Our lives can sometimes be solitary—but we can't get through life alone. It takes a team to support living in commitment, joy, generosity, and gratitude. Adventures companions can be actual people (or animals) that share the adventure with us and add more layers to the experience. Or they can be the natural elements we commune with—the ocean in surfing, the mountain in climbing, or the open road in driving.

Let's take a couple of somewhat typical—but not necessarily easy—scenarios and break down Walker's tenets of adventure.

Mountain-climbing is a high endeavor because it's simply a huge accomplishment, something that can prove a lot to yourself about what you can do. You have to commit to preparing diligently, knowing what to do and analyzing the terrain you'll cover. It's definitely got an uncertain outcome, especially if there's risk of an accident. You'll tolerate adversity because your mettle will be tested, and you'll likely have to make minor adjustments to your journey on the way. The great companionship could be expressed in an improved relationship with nature—or, if you don't do it alone, with whomever you go with.

Even a simple trip to another continent— *without* a guided tour—can incorporate all these elements. The endeavor is leaving your usual culture to experience something new and potentially different. You commit yourself to charting your own course through the trip without constant professional insistence. Almost all of your trip will be an uncertain outcome because you've opened yourself up to surprise. You might find adversity in being restricted in your communications with others because of the language difference. Even after all that, you might forge a bond with wherever you visit and the people who live there—the companionship.

The Similarities of These Approaches

What do all these methodologies have in common?

For one thing, they all express the importance of some kind of *commitment*. The three C's approach demands both conviction and clarity; you must know what you're doing and why you're doing it. The 2 AM principle sets down the need for agreements or even rules in its constraint component. Walker's model explicitly identifies commitment as its second definition.

These similarities imply that you need some kind of dedication to your efforts—even the fly-by bar hops that Levy describes. The commitment could be to effect change to amplify your personal abilities or just to find the best piña colada on Staten Island. That's on top of the additional, most obvious commitment to last through your entire adventure.

These methodologies also emphasize the elements of *surprise and the uncertain outcome*, which is at the heart of comfort zone busting. The clarity component of the three C's encourages you to find a positive affirmation in case the efforts don't turn out in your favor. Walker's model, again, directly mentions the uncertain outcome as not just a part of a great adventure, but something to be sought. Similarly, the 2 AM principle basically invites unpredictability at every opportunity; it's the lifeblood of Levy's formula.

Finally, all approaches account for *risks*. The three C's model is practically built on the admission of risk; each of its parts address what you have to do to get through tricky parts or potentially rough patches. The 2 AM principle instills risk as part of the program, and Walker's model partially defines adventure as facing adversity.

These three similarities actually give a pretty decent skeletal definition of what getting out of your comfort zone really means: something you *commit* to, in which you'll take certain *risks* for the sake of an *uncertain outcome*. That doesn't mean the adventure has to be grand in scale or dangerous—but it certainly means you can inject those elements into smaller social or personal events to *make* them adventurous.

Having a structured program or set of guidelines for getting outside your comfort zone gives you a roadmap for the uncharted territory you're about to take on. It comes preloaded with a context in which you can view your experiences and make them mean more—and then apply the lessons to your next steps away from the comfort zone.

Takeaways:

1. There are some established routines and methods for escaping the comfort zone and putting yourself in the position of new experiences and living fearlessly. The first method is the three C's method, which states that the comfort zone is best escaped with customization, clarity, and conviction.

2. The second method is Jon Levy's 2 AM principle, which is designed to help people seek more adventure and thrills. He also uses three elements: something is worthwhile for adventure if it is worth

talking about, it presents certain risks, and it makes you a different person after the fact.

3. Matt Walker's method involves five elements: thinking big, commitment, an uncertain outcome, tolerance for adversity, and companionship. It is worthwhile to examine what these three methods have in common, because no matter if your purpose is to extend your comfort zone or to altogether ditch it, it shows a fairly clear path.

Chapter 9. A Recipe for Adventure

If our comfort zone had windows, adventure is what we'd be seeing in the distance outside them while we're sitting in our recliner and slipping into solace. It's what provides what's possibly the only source of tension in the comfort zone: the fear that we're missing out on meaningful and scalable experiences that we're not going to get by staying home.

From that vantage point, it can be hard to conjure up what we need to break out and be more adventurous. We've got the methodologies in the previous chapter, but what about on a daily basis—how can we grab life by the neck and live boldly on a consistent basis?

We might start thinking we don't have the personal elements necessary to be bold and take those adventures. But in truth, the "tweaks" we'd have to make are comparatively minor—mainly in the area of attitude adjustment.

These ideas reflect some frames of mind we can coach ourselves into accepting, sort of to grease the wheels of the vehicle taking us out of the comfort zone.

Be a Little Crazy

Geniuses have the capability to change the world with their ideas and precepts. They have advanced the course of the Earth with bold ideas, new modes of thinking, and innovations.

They're also a little *nuts*. You can call it *eccentric* or *quirky*—they normally deviated from the norm in significant ways.

Take Albert Einstein, for instance. He radically transformed modern science with the theory of relativity. He also refused to wear socks and liked to go sailing on days when there was no wind.

Hunter S. Thompson ushered in a new style of journalism based on tenacity and calling out political nonsense. He also went searching for pygmies in a jungle and set fire to the America's Cup sailing trophy.

Why are geniuses more susceptible to being a little crazy? What made Einstein, Thompson, Vincent Van Gogh, Salvador Dali, and Prince such unmistakable masters but confirmed eccentrics? Rob Waugh, a reporter for the *Daily Mail*, thinks there's a scientific basis at work. "There *is* a link between creative genius and madness—with both schizophrenia and bipolar disorder frequent in highly creative and intelligent people."

A Swedish study on a group of 16-year-olds made some interesting connections. "They found that people who excelled when they were 16 years old were four times as likely to go on to develop bipolar disorder," says Kay Redfield Jamison of John Hopkins School of

Medicine, who suffers bipolar disorder. Students who excelled most had a specific gene—DARPP-32—which connects genius and mental instability. It actually improves the capacity to think.

The DARPP-32 gene is actually found in about 75% of all people. "The gene also shaped and controlled a nerve circuit, which links the prefrontal cortex with another brain region, the striatum, and is closely involved with schizophrenia," says Roger Highfield of the *Telegraph*.

The point being, we're all a bit crazy in different ways. On the fabled spectrum of human behavior, those with "mental illnesses" often lie on the extremes of it. Given that knowledge, we shouldn't be afraid to occasionally let the freak flag fly. That craziness lets us think from unique perspectives.

Don't stick to convention because you feel you'd stand out otherwise. Don't hold yourself or your actions back because you're afraid you'll look "weird." For one thing, "weirdness" is a lot more tolerated than it used to be. More people view it as an asset or at least a harmless trait. But remember the spotlight effect—chances are, what you do might not even register with others because nobody's *really* watching you.

On the other hand, *do* look for openings to inject levity into your lifestyle whenever you can—humor is an underrated but powerful tool. *Do* express yourself in whatever ways you see fit to reinforce your character while you're laying waste to comfort zones. *Do* embrace the odd, bizarre, and peculiar elements of your undertakings as if they were allies.

The quirks in your personality, the random detours of thought and crazy tangents you might go on, are what attracted your friends to you in the first place. They make you unique. They're what start the conversations and exchanges you have, and they invite adventure into your life that complements your own personality. They're what make your existence outside the comfort zone more relatable to you, because they're uniquely yours. You can't shake them whether you're in the comfort zone or not.

Create Your Own Momentum and Break Your Inertia

Comfort zones are made for still life. They're places where time and movement stop. But any meaningful activity involves breaking the inertia of the still life and generating momentum.

We perceive momentum as an outside force that attaches itself to our efforts; we don't have any control over it. That's simply not true. It's possible to produce our own momentum to get the wheels moving out of the comfort zone.

Give yourself three choices whenever you think about something:

- Schedule it for the very near future.

- Learn about it.

- Or DO it as soon as you can.

That's it. Those are your choices. End of discussion.

Well, I'll back it up a bit. What this strict limit of responses does is prevent the dreaded "analysis paralysis" from creating an unnecessary delay in your activity. It invites momentum to build. In that stream, you're more productive, more effective, and more efficient.

Momentum takes you over that first hurdle of not being able to start something due to your need to dissect, break down, and plan your actions in advance. It builds positive thinking and energy to move you toward you goal and makes you believe you can achieve whatever you want.

The first option—"schedule it in the very near future"—is intended to be reactive in case you just can't get to it right that instant. Put it on your docket and leave it until that time— just make sure you keep your schedule.

Learning about it is the option to choose if you think you need to find a little more information. This is not the same as analysis paralysis—this is active fact-finding, a basic investigation that will help tell you what to do, and not take you too deeply into the "weeds."

Doing it as soon as you can? That's self-explanatory. The sooner you can move on your thoughts, the sooner it changes your trajectory. And if you really have a driving impulse to start something now, and there's nothing preventing you from doing it, follow your instincts and set it to action.

Channel Your Seven-Your-Old Self

You might think there was never a time when breaking out of your comfort zone and seeking adventure was a regular way of thinking for you. You might believe that there's never been a time in your life when you were unfiltered and you weren't so self-conscious.

Try this. When you're sitting at your desk, surrounded by important information, open spreadsheets, a long list of pending items and pressing issues, and things you must get accomplished by the end of the day, ask yourself this extremely important question:

What would your seven-year-old self want to do right now?

I know if I was seven, I'd want to break out the crayons or the watercolors. Or I might want to go outside and run around for a bit, maybe take in some swing action. Or maybe a round of dress-up would be nice, or eating something with my hands, or playing that ukulele in the back of your closet that I haven't touched in years.

Just because you're grown up doesn't mean any of these examples will be less enjoyable than you remembered it. Even as we've become adults, these activities and attitudes remain effective ways to stir up creativity or just let off steam.

You're never too old to play—so give yourself permission to do it. Keep a sketchpad handy to doodle or draw (it might evolve into a pictorial solution). Give yourself a regularly scheduled recess during the day. Most of all, feel encouraged to question every aspect of your life, work, and surroundings the way a seven-year-old would question . . . well, just about everything. It never hurts to approach life from an innocent standpoint, because the most intelligent of us humans knows that learning never stops.

Our comfort zone is strapped with beliefs, behaviors, and attitudes that we've largely learned as teenagers or older. We believe maturation is a linear and intractable process that we must never veer away from. But that's largely a product of our own self-consciousness, a vision we feel we must live up to, and our comfort zone filters out elements we think might be foolish, childish, or callow. To break out of that way of thinking, just for a while, try to approach parts of your life as if you were seeing them for the first time—and acting like a child. Try to let your sense of curiosity and wonderment carry you into uncharted waters.

Understand Your Constraints and Barriers

The way we approach the edge of the comfort zone is a big part of the recipe for personal, daily adventure. Simply, how do we tend to deal with hurdles in our way? It turns out there are some patterns people tend to adhere to, so it would behoove you to understand where you fall on the spectrum.

In their book *A Beautiful Constraint*, Adam Morgan and Mark Braden share three mindsets we fall into when we deal with constraints. When a certain condition is thrust into our pathway to a given accomplishment, there are three behavioral categories that inform our responses and intentions.

To describe these facets, consider the example of a small-business baker who's looking to move his bakery to a bigger place. They've found the perfect property in a great location but discover that the rent is prohibitively expensive.

There are three stances the baker could take:

Victim. When someone lowers their ambition when faced with a constraint, they play into the mindset of a victim. "I'll just can't do it," the baker would say. "I can't move right now because the time isn't right."

Neutralizer. This is someone who refuses to lower the ambition but finds alternative ways to deliver it. The neutralizer is resilient but devises new strategies to work around constraints. In this mode the baker would say, "I must have this store . . . but maybe I can also start a website to expand the business and offset the rent increase."

Transformer. This type tries to turn constraints into opportunity and might increase their own ambition in the process. When the transformer faces a loss, they leverage the situation as an opportunity to rethink the business. "I don't need a physical store!" the transformer baker would say. "I'll just sell online or send baked goods as part of a subscription!"

Each story the baker could tell shapes their attitude, and their behavior follows suit. It's a self-fulfilling prophecy. Whatever they believe about their options determines what they'll do and ultimately the outcome of their efforts.

The victim mindset just doesn't handle the adventure angle very well. They see their existence as a result of transgressions the world has made upon them, and they just have to take their lumps and withdraw.

The neutralizer has a little more aspiration. They consider the possibility of adventure and might have realistic ways to attain it. It doesn't have to happen right now, but after a little work or setup, it could happen soon.

The transformer, obviously, either jumps over the hurdles immediately or just kicks them out of the damn way. It's almost like the adventure chases after *them*. They see the ability to shape events to their own will as a natural state of being.

So which are you, and how might that contribute to your daily adventure? There is one category (the transformer) that tends to experience more adventure, while the others tend to stay trapped behind obstacles and boundaries.

All of those personas can be outside the comfort zone and survive (even the victim).

But figuring out what role we most often take in certain situations can be a big step in help to thrive when we're under challenges and need to take action. We may still be in our comfort zones because we don't really *know* which of these personas we are. Figuring out where we stand is the first part in almost anything. Leaving the comfort zone is no different.

Takeaways:

1. Be a little bit crazy in only the way you know how. In other words, be your unique self and don't fall back in line when you deviate from the norm. It's this unique insight that will illuminate your path to adventure.

2. Seek momentum and destroy inertia by taking immediate action on information you care about: learn about it, schedule it, or do it instantly. For many people, planning and rumination is actually counterproductive.

3. Listen to your seven-year old self—they had some good ideas and didn't have any filters about them.

4. Understand what happens when you come across constraints and barriers, as there are three typical types of reactions: victim, neutralizer, and transformer. The transformer category kicks obstacles out of the way and thus doesn't let anything deter their path out of the comfort zone.

Summary Guide

Chapter 1. What Zone Do You Live In?

- The comfort zone is certainly real, but only as far as you believe in it. That is to say, it is purely mental, and as such, something you can get around.

- The Yerkes–Dodson curve is a representation of how the comfort zone affects our performance and just why it is so important to step outside and expose yourself to optimal levels of stress. It also demonstrates the importance of pacing yourself and making sure to stay in your comfort zone from time to time for recovery, not rest.

- The brain likes staying in the comfort zone for the lack of stressors, but we are actually physiologically rewarded for experiencing novelty and thrills. You are happier outside of your comfort zone in the end.

- The regret minimization framework implores you to ask what you'll regret not doing at the age of 80. This sidesteps perceived obstacles and simply asks what you want to do without regard to your fears or anxieties.

Chapter 2. Comfort-Destroying Mindsets

- Breaking the comfort zone begins with the mindsets you have about leaving it in the first place. The first mindset to overcome is that of catastrophizing—the feeling that everything is falling apart at any moment. This is driven by a skewed and fearful approach.

- The next mindset is to assess risk better and more accurately. We stay in the comfort zone because we feel everything is too risky. Similar to catastrophizing, this makes us prone to inaction. We assess risk emotionally when it should be placed in more grounded terms.

- We don't leave the comfort zone because we feel a need to be in control of what happens to us. Of course, anything new or novel is inherently outside of our control because we don't know it. Our mindsets must become more comfortable with change, novelty, and a lack of control over everything.

- What would your seven-year old self want to do? They were fearless, without filter, and gave no regard as to potential risks or fears. This is whom you might want to channel more frequently.

Chapter 3. Breaking Your Beliefs

- If you want to leave the comfort zone, you must first believe that you can indeed do it. The first way to instill that belief is to understand how many different types of courage exist and how many you might exhibit that aren't the traditional ones you can fixate on. You can leave the comfort zone; you just have to find your own avenue to do it.

- The spotlight effect can be crippling. If we imagine that every one of our actions is dissected under a microscope, we might never do anything. But it's also a cognitive malfunction that is almost always incorrect.

- Defense mechanisms are some of the nastiest barriers to leaving the comfort zone because they act to protect your ego. To protect your ego, you don't attempt to do anything you have a chance in failing at. The most common defense mechanisms are rationalization, denial, and intellectualization.

- Aside from defense mechanisms, we might have beliefs about ourselves or the world that have been ingrained in us since childhood. They are largely unconscious until you examine the deep bases for your opinions and beliefs. They usually don't hold up under evidence or scrutiny.

Chapter 4. Run Before You're Ready

- Perfectionism isn't just procrastination; perfectionism is a story you tell yourself to ensure that you never get launched. But let's face the facts: your standards aren't the issue. It's your unwillingness to subject yourself to scrutiny from others.

- Planning paralysis is when you become enamored with the preparation and planning as another form of procrastination that ultimately allows you to avoid action. It's sneaky!

- The 40–70 rule states that you should have no fewer than 40% of the necessary information yet no more than 70% before taking action or making a hard decision. This errs on the side of action but also ensures that you aren't just shooting from the hip.

- Action is preferred, but action is scary. Therefore, part of the assurance you can make to yourself in taking action is to actively think about the costs for backing out and reversing decisions.

Chapter 5. Stay on Your Toes

- Breaking out of your comfort zone is an exercise in discomfort and pain. Therefore, we should exercise the mental muscles involved in dealing with such feelings.

- Stoicism represents the first method to deal with discomfort because they encouraged practicing voluntary discomfort. They believed that fear was rooted in a lack of experience; therefore, exposure to all manners of discomfort would make one more resilient and immune to negative emotions. This makes your comfort zone grow exponentially.

- Similarly, feeling and resisting urges at least twice before giving in is a practice in discipline and discomfort.

- Finally, becoming comfortable with flexibility and spontaneity is important because of the lack of control. If you can become accustomed to the feeling of controlled chaos by utilizing techniques such as randomness, eliminating "wrong" beliefs, and not saying no out of habit, you'll become far more likely to say "so what?" and break out of your comfort zone.

Chapter 6. Create an Alter Ego

- The power of an alter ego has been shown in studies on online anonymity. If you can be vile and rude online as someone else, imagine the positive potential of anonymity.

- Your alter ego, to be most effective, should represent your ideal self, at least in the aspect of breaking out of your comfort zone. What do you wish you were more or less of? What traits are you seeking? That's what your alter ego should epitomize because you already know what *you'll* do in certain situations and it's something you want to change.

- The alter ego serves as a buffer and counter to the ego—Freud's concept of what keeps us insulated from judgment and rejection.

- The best alter egos are highly defined and detailed and also have an activation element—there must be a signal to snap you into your alter ego, so to speak. This is important because otherwise there is no way to easily disassociate from your everyday persona.

Chapter 7. Mission: Impossible

- We're all normal, yet normal people appear to do the impossible or frightening every day. So what's it to you? Your turn is coming.

- A large part of what holds us back are the limiting beliefs about our abilities. This can be easily shown when creating an "I can't do" list. Adding a "but" statement at the

216

end is a powerful way to show that you can indeed do something, just not to the arbitrary standard you were holding yourself to. It is direct evidence that it is not impossible or even scary.

- Carrots and sticks are important in the sense that they can decimate a comfort zone by themselves. Carrots are positive reinforcers, while sticks are negative reinforcers—essentially rewards and punishments, respectively. If you can be clear enough about what motivates you from both aspects—negative and positive—you just might have enough to bypass your fears and doubts.

Chapter 8. Comfort Zone Busting Methodologies

- There are some established routines and methods for escaping the comfort zone and putting yourself in the position of new experiences and living fearlessly. The first method is the three C's method, which states that the comfort zone is best escaped with customization, clarity, and conviction.

- The second method is Jon Levy's 2 AM principle, which is designed to help people seek more adventure and thrills. He also uses three elements: something is worthwhile for adventure if it is worth talking about, it presents certain risks, and it makes you a different person after the fact.

- Matt Walker's method involves five elements: thinking big, commitment, an uncertain outcome, tolerance for adversity, and companionship. It is worthwhile to examine what these three methods have in common, because no matter if your purpose is to extend your comfort zone or to altogether ditch it, it shows a fairly clear path.

Chapter 9. A Recipe for Adventure

- Be a little bit crazy in only the way you know how. In other words, be your unique self and don't fall back in line when you deviate from the norm. It's this unique insight that will illuminate your path to adventure.

- Seek momentum and destroy inertia by taking immediate action on information you care about: learn about it, schedule it, or do it instantly. For many people, planning and rumination is actually counterproductive.

- Listen to your seven-year old self—they had some good ideas and didn't have any filters about them.

- Understand what happens when you come across constraints and barriers, as there are three typical types of reactions: victim, neutralizer, and transformer. The transformer category kicks obstacles out of the way and thus doesn't let anything deter their path out of the comfort zone.

26770539R00125

Printed in Poland
by Amazon Fulfillment
Poland Sp. z o.o., Wrocław